TSUMITATE INVESTMENT

Lucrative even at half price

Yasuhira Hoshino

Table of contents

Title
Copyrights
Acknowledgment
Foreword   1
About the Author   11

Chapter 1
"Relief from falling prices" Effect: No matter how low the price falls   **13**

Case 1: Even at half price   13
Case 2: Even after dipping to 10¢   15
Lesson From Life 1: Peace of Mind is Paramount   17

Chapter 2
"Rapid recovery" Effect: Rapid recovery from losses   **18**

Case 3: When is the recovery?   18
Lesson From Life 2: Bouncing Back after Failing is Important   20

Chapter 3
"Rebound" Effect: Gain returns if bouncing back after a drop   **22**

Case 4: Return to original level   22
Lesson From Life 3: Squatting to Jump High   24

Chapter 4
"Increasing price" Effect: Automatic investing vs. Lump-sum investing   **25**

Case 5: When it doubles   25
Case 6: Going up, then dipping a little   26
Case 7: Return to original price   27
Lesson From Life 4: Good Balance is Crucial   28

Chapter 5
"No timing" Effect: Don't worry about when to start 29

Case 8: When should I start?   29
Case 9: When should I start? (2)   30
Lesson From Life 5: Act Without Fear   32

Chapter 6
"Ending" Effect: Knowing when to stop is extremely
important   33

Case 10: Knowing when to stop is important   33
Lesson From Life 6: If the end result is good, it was all
worthwhile   35

Chapter 7
"Process" Effect: It is important to watch prices in the
process, as well as those at the start and end.   36

Case 11: Even if your goals are the same   36
Case 12: The process is important   37
Lesson From Life 7: Result or Process   38

Chapter 8
"Continuity" Effect: Quitters never win   39

Case 13: If periods vary   39

Lesson From Life 8: Endurance Makes You Stronger   40

Chapter 9
"Slow increase" Effect: Slow, rather than rapid, increases
41

Case 14: Slow increases   41
Case 15: What if it jumps 100 fold?   42
Lesson From Life 9: Sometimes Slower is Better   44

Chapter 10
"No predicting" Effect: I don't remember putting any thought into it
45

Case 16: Vertically symmetric   45
Case 17: 8 zigzag funds   46
Case 18: Another 8 zigzag funds   47
Lesson From Life 10: Act Without Worry   48

Chapter 11
Conclusion: What is tsumitate investing?
49

List of tsumitate investing effects   49
Conclusion   50

Appendix A: Messages from Japanese Financial Sector
53

Appendix B: Messages from Japanese Financial Planners and Bloggers
75

Appendix C: Date Summary   90
Appendix D: Translator Profile   92

ACKNOWLEDGMENTS

This booklet is the product of over 100,000 verifications and would not have been possible without the help of others. It came to be thanks to the efforts of literally scores of individuals including many friends and colleagues, all of them key figures in the Japanese financial sector. This message is not only from me, but from the entire financial industry of Japan.

I would like to take this opportunity to express my appreciation for all those who supported me throughout, and I would be truly honored if this booklet contributed to the asset formation of people around the world.

Kazuhisa Okamoto
Atsuto Sawakami
Satoshi Nojiri
Ken Shibusawa
Hideto Fujino
Koichi Ito
Yasuyuki Kamata
Akinori Kamiji
Shinji Kimura
Choongdo Kang, SINYO FP Office
Kenichi Minase, A Random Walk Down Umeyashiki Street
Blogger "PET", Your Own Boss (Asset Management Blog)
mushitorikozou
Shunsuke Ito, Discussion on KYOUGOKU DEMACHI
Financial Planner
Tooru Ushiroda,"The Life Insurance Trap"
Blogger "Rakutenkagyou"
Blogger "TravelBookCafe"
Blogger "yako"
Blogger"I-no", An Ocean of Funds
Blogger "renny"
Blogger "Leverage", Leveraged Investment Diary
pockypocky

Blogger "m@"
Ryota Ito, Financial Planner
Blogger "taka"
Blogger "Jyuuichiya"
Blogger "makiko"
Masaki Otani
John L. Clark

FOREWORD

1.What is tsumitate investing?

I refer to investing continuously on a monthly basis as "tsumitate." This word is Japanese for "accumulation." The Merriam-Webster© dictionary defines "accumulation" as "increase or growth by addition especially when continuous or repeated." This means never quit, and make every effort to keep piling on little by little. This is one of the values held dear by Japanese people for centuries.

Tsumitate investing is not a way to use your present amount of money like you have in a bank account. It's the way to use the future money you will earn from a salary or other income.

Present Amount Of Money
―Future money

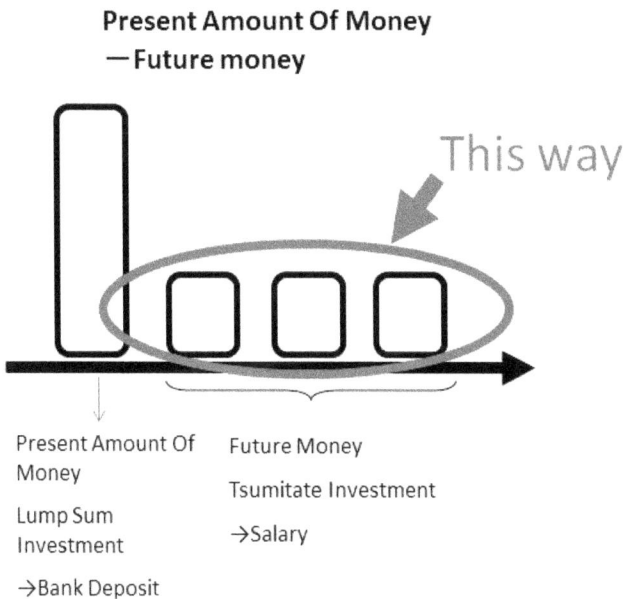

This way

Present Amount Of Money

Lump Sum Investment

→Bank Deposit

Future Money

Tsumitate Investment

→Salary

Tsumitate investing is the easiest way of investment that anyone can do simply because it involves the accumulation of small amounts bit by bit. This is particularly great for company employees who are finding it more and more difficult to divert their savings toward investments. But anyone can invest a little money from their monthly salary.

What I am trying to do here is shed light on the qualities of tsumitate investing, which is easy to start for most people but is the least understood.

An important point to remember is that tsumitate investing is not completely faultless. There are good and bad aspects to it. It's good because it relieves stress, and it's bad because you won't get rich from it. It is essential to understand its characteristics, together with lump-sum investments, and use it to build an investment strategy that matches your life goals.

To do this you must first understand its character. This booklet is the first attempt to describe in detail the advantages and disadvantages of tsumitate investing.

2.Features that have never been fully explained in the past

Investing continuously on a monthly basis is called various names: Automatic Investment, Dollar-Cost Averaging, Systematic Investment, etc. Such plans are well-known and have penetrated markets all over the world. In the U.S., 401K corporate pension plans, IRAs and other schemes allow many Americans to use tsumitate investing as a way to form their future assets.

You'll probably find it surprising, but this type of investment has never been fully explained to the public. Its features can be summed up in one phrase: "The results of the product you invested in do not match the results of your investment." Buying into a good product every month does not absolutely guarantee favorable results.

Why hasn't this important point ever been revealed? The reason is that the financial industry has never really put any effort into researching tsumitate investing simply because it doesn't provide short-term wealth. Over the last several years, I made tens of thousands of verifications that resulted in the systematization of the features for continuous monthly investment, which have never been fully explained before.

3. Why explaining tsumitate investing is necessary

The life expectancy of people all over the world is increasing. As life-spans become longer, it is increasingly important to plan for old age. The future world will require that each and every one of us have their own retirement nest egg.

Tsumitate investing is the easiest way for people to accumulate future assets. Explaining the features of this type of investment will contribute to the asset formation of people all over the world.

This booklet shows how tsumitate investing works by comparing it with "lump-sum investment" where substantial amounts are invested all at once. This will not merely be knowledge to you, but a tool that will help you think when its time to invest.

4. Belief that lower prices mean losses

"Losing money when the price falls"

Most folks probably think this is common sense. In my many years as a mutual fund salesman, I would always encounter customers who thought they were losing money when prices fell.

Certainly, if you invest all your money at one time, you will lose money if the price goes down. But this is not necessarily the case if you invest continuously every single month.

5. Even at half price

Have a look at the graph below. It shows the price movement of a certain investment fund over 10 years. Let's call it "Fund A."

Price: $

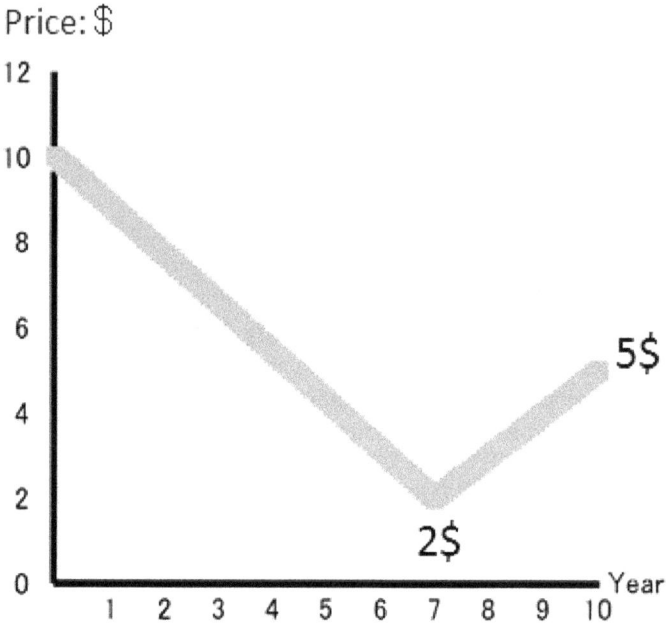

The starting price was $10. Over a 7-year period, it went down to $2 and jumped back up again. At the 10-year mark, it was at $5. Half price over 10 years. Unfortunately, if you had invested in Fund A at the beginning and waited 10 years, your asset would have lost half its value.

However, if you had continually invested a fixed amount every month over that 10-year period, what do think would have happened? Investing monthly means that you invest 12 times in 1-year period. Over 10 years, that's 120 investments. If you had invested 120 times every single month, would you have been in the red? Or would you have been in black?

The correct answer is "PROFIT"!

Even if the price is half what it was when you started, if you had invested on a monthly basis, you would have made a profit.

4

People who believed that when investing a fall in prices results in losses will probably be surprised, but it's true that in this case, a tsumitate investment will result in a profit even at half price.

I'll provide the details later on, but for now, please understand that with monthly investments made automatically, even if the price goes down lower than what it was at the start, that doesn't necessarily mean you'll suffer a loss. You may even make money like in the above example with Fund A.

Such continuous, monthly investments have various aspects that are contrary to our usual understanding of investing. Consider the next Case.

6. Don't worry about when to start

This graph also shows the price movement of one investment fund. If you plan to invest continually every month for 10 years, from which point in time, either A, B, C, D or E, do you have to start to make the most money?

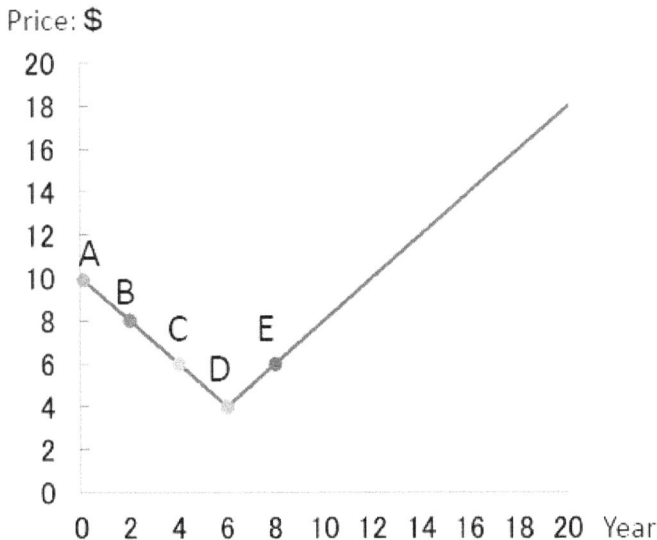

Price: $

20	
18	
16	
14	
12	A
10	B
8	C E
6	D
4	
2	
0	

0 2 4 6 8 10 12 14 16 18 20 Year

If you think you should start at the point with the lowest price, then "D" should be your answer. But actually "C" is correct. The order from most profitable to least profitable is C→D→B→E→A. Do you know why C is better than D, and B is better than E?

I will also explain this later, but the bottom-line is that if you plan to continue to invest every month, it doesn't matter when you start and you don't have to worry about waiting for the lowest price.

7. Vertically symmetric funds

Let's try another one. Look at the graph below. The starting price for both A and B is $10. Over 7 years, A went up to $18 but then decreased to $15 at the 10-year mark. So it increased in value by 50% over 10 years. On the other hand, B fell to a value of $2 over 7 years and then shot up finishing at $5 after 10 years. Its value went down 50% over a decade. If you look at the graph, you'll see that the price movement of A and B are vertically symmetric.

Price: $

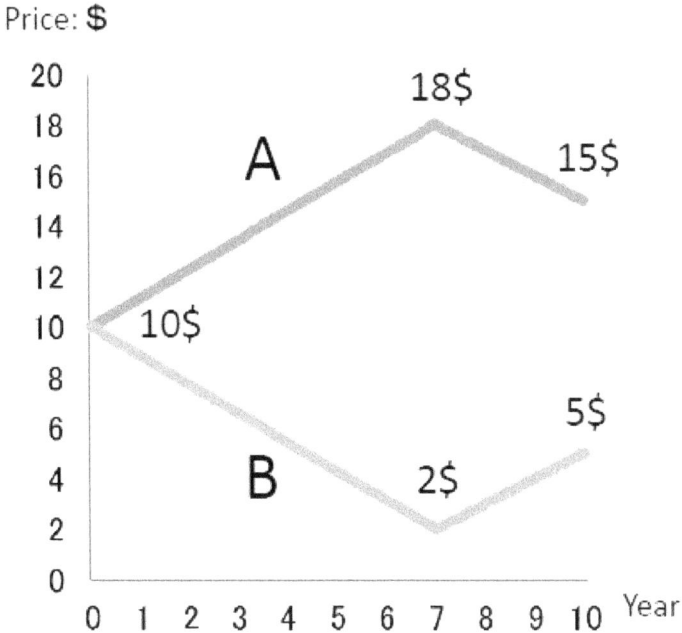

If I ask you to choose between financial product A and B in terms of highest profit from start to finish, you'd probably pick A, right? Well, A is the correct answer because its gave investors a 50% profit over the investment period, while those who invested in B lost half their equity.

Now if I ask you the same thing only in terms of continuous investments of a fixed amount every month over 10 years, which one would you pick?

The correct answer is B. Yes, B, whose price fell to half its starting value, is more profitable than A. Even though the graph lines of A and B are vertically symmetric and A is the clear winner in terms of mutual fund performance.

Such investments when done constantly on a monthly basis, are quite different from conventional investments. This is what I'm trying to explain.

8. Support from Japan's financial sector

This booklet was possible thanks in great part to key players such as Japanese asset management company administrators, scholars, analysts and fund managers. I received over 10 letters of commendation from such individuals. Until now, no Japanese has ever written a book about investing for publication overseas. This is the very first of its kind in Japan to be sent out to the world.

Born in December 1981, I was 29 years old when I wrote this booklet. These famous individuals have much longer careers in the financial industry than me, wrote many books and enjoy an elevated status in society. I am very happy to have obtained their valuable support.

Why is it that these remarkable people lent me a hand? It's probably because they feel as I do that diffusing the qualities of tsumitate investing to the world is of paramount importance. Think for a moment of all those industry leaders encouraging the diffusion of a message from your young friends. This is not a question of age difference, but rather a shared purpose. I believe I can take this message overseas to America and other countries for the benefit of all people.

9. People who will benefit from this booklet

This booklet will help a variety of people. Those who already started their 401K or IRA should learn how their own investments will be affected by changes in the market. With tsumitate investing, a sharp decline in the market at the end of an investment period could result in grave circumstances for the investor. On the other hand, such downward trends could be ignored or rather welcomed with open arms. And just because the price goes up, that doesn't necessarily mean you'll make money. It's essential to understand these features well.

Tsumitate investing is also good for people planning to start their 401Ks or IRAs. If they can understand the features of the investments to make for their retirement, they won't be afraid of the numerous market downfalls that might be expected along the way.

Companies with 401K plans for their employees should consider using this booklet as a new learning tool for retirement-geared investment. Asset allocation and compound interest calculation are important concepts that most people already know about. But tsumitate investing is not that well-known yet.

This booklet contains details that would be very useful to financial advisers and planners. They could even hold seminars to follow up on their clients' investments. Distributing information not provided by anyone else will differentiate you from the other advisers and planners and earn you more trust from clients. The complete content
of this booklet is available free of charge on my website:
http://tsumitate-investment.com.

Please use it as much as possible. Others like you in Japan have already made use of it in their business.
Financial institutions could also use it for marketing purposes. I'm sure your customers would be happy to obtain information they've never heard before. In Japan, several financial institutions are already distributing it to their customers.

10.Changing the image of investing

"Lower prices mean losses"

The entire world believes it and we should all work together to try to change this way of thinking. To achieve this, let's tell everybody about tsumitate investing. Investors around the globe will be surprised and happy to hear about it. Let's tell them all about the wonders of investing.

Unfortunately, tsumitate investing is facing a large obstacle: There are not enough people to spread out the message. It is not being pushed by the financial industry because it doesn't earn lots of money over a short period of time. For all of you who, after reading this booklet, feel they would like to teach people about the merits of tsumitate investing, let's pool our strengths and diffuse the message together. Let's make tsumitate investing common knowledge for everyone.

Only you can change the image of investing.

Yasuhira Hoshino

About the Author

Mr. Tsumitate
Yasuhira Hoshino

Born in 1981 and graduated Faculty of Economics, Shinshu University.
Joined Nippon Investors Securities Co., Ltd., as the third largest shareholder individually with capital participation, and appointed the youngest in that company to be given the position "Kyushu Area Manager."

While there, instead of upholding the same approach prevalent throughout the financial industry of targeting seniors and wealthy individuals, I focused my research on small-sum "tsumitate investing" plans that even young people my age can buy into. I made over 100,000 verifications and succeeded in systematizing the characteristics of dollar-cost averaging, a method never fully expounded in conventional finance.

In the summer of 2009, that company was sold and I became independent. At the end of 2010, Kodansha, the largest publisher in Japan, published my book "Tsumitate investing: Lucrative even at half price" in Japanese. It impacted the market the moment it hit the shelves and over the next 2 months, 70 reviews were done by financial bloggers and 2 additional printings were ordered to satisfy demand. Since then, I've appeared on several media outlets multiple times and gave lectures, wrote publications and conducted training seminars at financial institutions.

My graphs describing the features of tsumitate investing were lauded by the Japanese financial industry as "never-before-seen content," and asset management company administrators, analysts, university professors, fund managers, think tank researchers, media editors and a number of other key Japanese financial sector players support my activities. Lastly, I will be the first in Japan to publish overseas in the finance genre.

My dream is to share the qualities of tsumitate investing with people all over the world. My website provides free of charge all of my research content for people who agree with me and share my way of thinking. I hope to contribute to the asset formation of people around the globe.

Contact
Mail: yasuhirahoshino[at]gmail.com (at→@)

HP
English: http://tsumitate-investment.com/
Japanese: http://yasuhoshi.me/

Twitter
English: @tsumitate
Japanese: @yasuhoshi
Facebook
http://www.facebook.com/pages/tsumitate-investmentcom/128490117197332

Chapter 1 "Relief from falling prices" Effect: No matter how low the price falls

With tsumitate investing, you don't have to fear falling prices. Even if the price goes down to half its original value, that doesn't mean you'll suffer a loss. I'll explain why you can have peace of mind even in times of falling prices.

Case 1: Even at half price

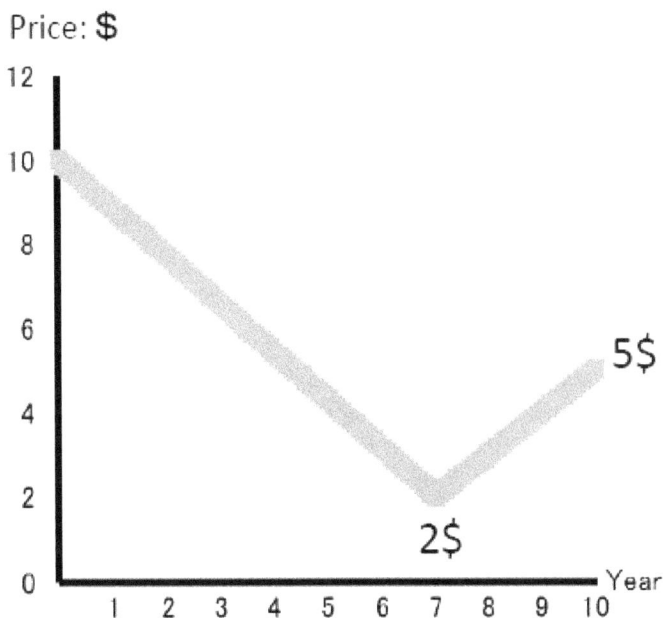

Price: $

Here, the starting price is $10. It went down to $2 over 7 years and jumped back up 3 years later to $5. The end price is half the value of the starting price. If you had invested only once at the beginning and waited 10 years, you would have lost half your money. Now what would have happened if you had invested every month? $100 per month makes $1,200 over a year, and 10 years later you get $12,000, right? What if you invest the same amount every single month in this fund with its price movements over the investment period, what would have happened to your $12,000?

1. $7,200   2. $9,000 or 3. $13,900

What do you think? The correct answer is 3! Even if the fund value decreases by half, you still make a profit. That's tsumitate investing! If you had put the same $12,000 in the fund all at once at the beginning and waited 10 years, you would have ended up with $6,000. But you're in the black with tsumitate investing...do you know why?

Tsumitate Investing Formula

Use the formula below to help you visualize tsumitate investing. You'll understand all the previous answers.

Investment Value = Amount x Price

Investing involves "purchasing" a financial instrument whose value is the result of multiplying the "amount" you purchased by the price of that instrument. For example, if you have 100 apples at $1 each, the "value" of all the apples is $1 x 100, or $100.

Normally, investments are made by focusing our attention on "how much it costs," or the "price" of the financial instrument, and almost never does anyone think about the "amount," the number of units purchased.

Under normal conditions when a single investment is made, the amount initially purchased does not change. Haven't you always thought about just the price when considering an investment? You probably never viewed investing from the perspective of "what amount should I buy?"

Tsumitate investing entails investing on a monthly basis. The price of a mutual fund changes every month so the amount of that fund you purchase is also different depending on the price in any given month. When the price of a product you invest in is low, you can purchase many units, and when the price is high, you purchase less.

Therefore, in the case we just saw, the more the price goes down, the higher the amount we can buy. Particularly when the price was at $2, its lowest point 7 years after the start of the investment period, the highest number of units of that fund was purchased.

What happens later when the price goes up? The amount of units you accumulated is valued at a higher price and the value of your investment increases.

For example, the value of your 100 apples bought at $1 each is $100, right? But if the price goes up to $2, then the value doubles to $200. The price of the product goes up, so the value of investment also goes up.

In this case, the price was half what it was at the start. However, because a high amount was purchased over the investment period, multiplying it by that ending price would result in a profit.

Case 2: Even after dipping to 10¢

Price: $

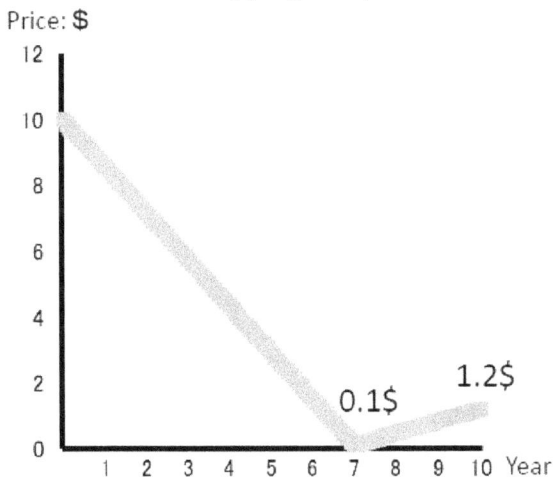

Let's try another one. It's an extreme case. Although you won't find such a case in your actual life, think of it as part of your training to understand the investment. The starting price was $10 and 7 years later, the price plummeted to 10¢. Then 3 years later at the 10-year mark of the investment period, the price recovered to $1.20, an 88% decrease in value from start to finish. If you had invested $100 monthly in this fund with such price fluctuations, what would have happened to your total $12,000 investment?

1. $5,300   2. $9,800   3. $14,500

What do you think? The answer is 3! Even after losing as much as 88%, the fund provided a profit of over 20%. Let's compare that with the previous case. It's surprising that this one makes us more money than the previous one.

With tsumitate investing, you should never think that a lower price automatically results in losses. This is very different from normal investments which are judged based only on price fluctuations. Tsumitate investing provides a chance to purchase more when the price goes down. Subsequent increases in price would result in a handsome profit.

This is an effect called "relief from falling prices" not present in usual lump-sum investments. No matter how low it gets, if it recovers to some value at the end, you won't lose. With tsumitate investing, you'll get peace of mind no matter how low the price falls.

The human brain is sensitive to losses

The human brain is programmed to react more strongly when faced with loss than with gain. For example, if you could flip a coin where heads wins you $10,000 and tails makes you pay out $10,000, would you do it? Most people would probably be scared of getting tails.

According to Princeton University Professor Daniel Kahneman, who won the Nobel Prize for Economics, our brains react 2 to 2.5 times more to "loss" stimuli than to "profit."

In the world of asset management, nobody can predict the future. We may see another big market collapse in a couple of years. Investors are constantly worried about the possibility of falling prices.

Tsumitate investing alleviates this fear and provides a relief effect when faced with falling prices. This is a huge advantage for investors.

Cautions

Just now I described an extreme case where the price crashed to 10¢ in order to help explain the features of tsumitate investing. Before starting such an investment plan, you should be cautious of the other elements involved. If this had been an individual company, the likelihood of bankruptcy when the stock price tanked to 10¢ is much greater than that of a recovery.

From a risk management perspective, the safest bet is a mutual fund where you can invest in multiple companies all at once.

Lesson From Life 1: Peace Of Mind Is Paramount

In all things, peace of mind is top priority. When buying food, do you select dubious items just because they're cheap? Do you live in a broken down house just because the rent is low? People will most likely choose on the basis of peace of mind in all things. Tsumitate investing provides this peace of mind.

Chapter 2 "Rapid recovery" Effect: Rapid recovery from losses

With tsumitate investing, even if you suffer a temporary loss, you can recover quickly into the black. In other words, tsumitate investing has the "power to recuperate."

Case 3: When is the recovery?

Price: $

12
10
8
6
4
2
0

① ② ③ 10$

2$

1 2 3 4 5 6 7 8 9 10 Year

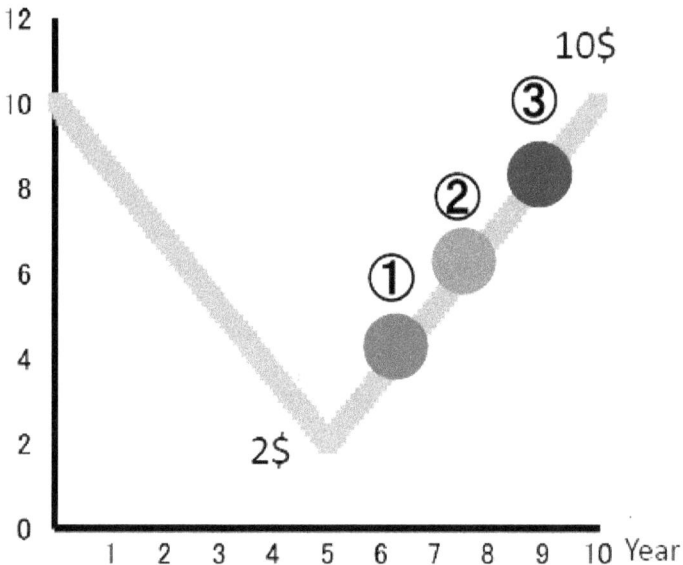

The investment started at $10 and fell to $2 at the 5-year mark. With a steady, monthly "tsumitate" investment, you would suffer about a 60% loss at this low point. The fund goes back up to its original price of $10 over the remaining 5 years of the investment period and starts becoming profitable at some point during that time. Between the 5-year and 10-year mark, when did the fund start making money for the investor?

1. After 6 years and 6 months
2. After 7 years and 10 months
3. After 8 years and 9 months

Which one? The answer is 1. After 6 years and 6 months, or 18 months from the bottom, the fund became profitable.

With tsumitate investing, if the price returns to a certain level after a decrease, you automatically make money. In a lump-sum investment, if the price does not return to its original level, there is no recovery in value. However, tsumitate investing is the quickest way to see a recovery. This is called the "rapid recovery" effect of tsumitate investing.

Why does tsumitate investing allow you to recover your losses so fast? Take another look at the formula.

Investment Value = Amount x Price

With tsumitate investing, you can buy a large amount when the price goes down. That's why when the price increases, you recover your losses.

Actually, this "rapid recovery" effect is the same as the "relief from falling prices" effect I described earlier. I described the latter effect from the perspective of "price," that is, relief no matter how low the price falls. Whereas, the rapid recovery effect was presented from a "time" perspective which means you can rapidly recover from losses. Either one ultimately lets you buy a lot of units effectively when the price goes down.

Example using the Dow Jones Industrial Average

Let's look at a specific example. The graph below shows the movement of the Dow Jones Industrial Average from the end of October 2007 to the end of December 2010 during which the global financial crisis resulted in a sharp decline in stock prices.

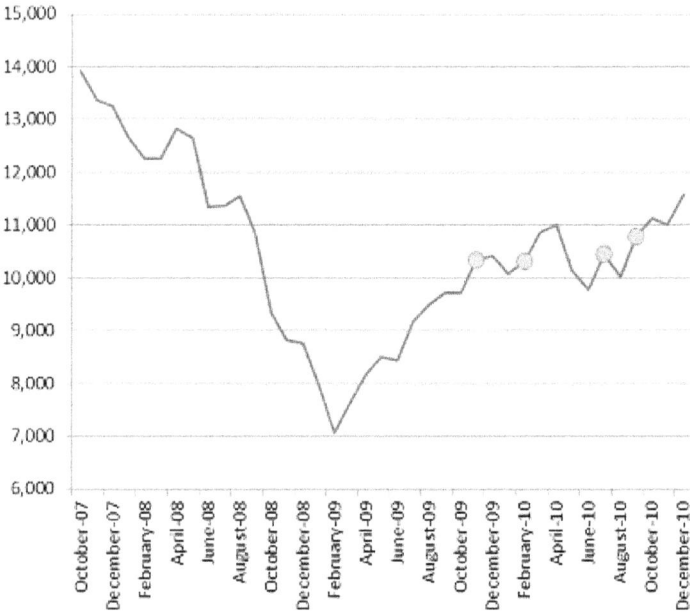

People who had invested a lump-sum at the end of October 2007 had about a 17% deficit at the end of the period. So what happened to tsumitate investors during this time? The answer is a 13.6% profit! Even with no recovery in price, investors were in the black.

Take a look at the dots along the line in the chart. These are markers showing the points investors made a profit... 4 times during the period! This is the rapid recovery effect tsumitate investing provides even when prices fall.

Lesson From Life 2: Bouncing Back after Failing is Important

Everyone has failed at some point in their lives. But it is through such failures that people learn. This is also true of tsumitate investing. When the price goes down, so does the value. But then a rapid recovery is all that is needed to get that value back.

What's important in life as well as investing is the "power to recuperate."

Chapter 3 "Rebound" Effect:
Gains return when bouncing back after a drop

Tsumitate investing provides profit after a drop in price only by having it return to its original level. That's called the "rebound" effect.

Case 4: Return to original level

Price: $

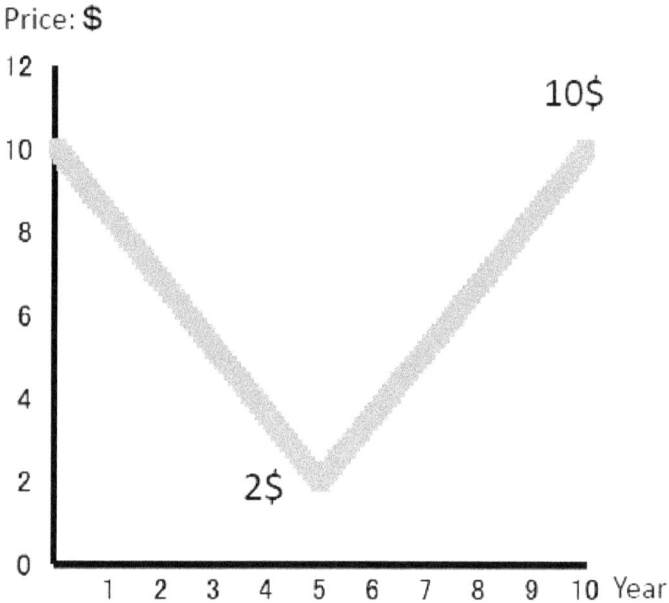

This is the same as the last example. The starting price is $10, It went down to $2 after 5 years and recovered back to the original price 5 years later at the 10-year mark. After 10 years, the price went back to its original level. In the case of a tsumitate investment of $100 a month with a total invested amount of $12,000, what would be the result?

1. $15,000   2. $19,600   3. $24,100

What do you think? The answer is 3! The invested amount doubled thanks only to a recovery in price to its original level. This is the "rebound" effect of tsumitate investing, which provides profit after falling prices just by having it go back to its starting point.

Why is that? Why do we make a profit only with the price back to where it started? Look again at the formula:

Investment Value = Amount x Price

Is it clear now? Because you can buy a large amount when the price is low, all it has to do is go up again to where it started for you to make a profit. This formula helps you understand the qualities of tsumitate investing.

With lump-sum investments, periods of falling prices are times when you have to endure. This is no fun. On the other hand, such periods in tsumitate investments are times of "anticipatory investing" in preparation for when prices will jump back up. The more the price goes down, the more you look forward to future upturns.

Tsumitate Investing vs. Weight Training

With tsumitate investing, periods of falling prices can be thought of as weight training for an athlete. He or she trains with weights to strengthen muscles. Providing nutrition and rest to muscle fibers bruised by weight training makes them a bit stronger than before. The more you train, the stronger your muscles get.

With tsumitate investing, units are bought up when the market is down. Those acquired at low prices create a surge in the value of your investment when the market goes back up.

As in weight training, tsumitate investing provides benefits after going through difficult times. The longer the tunnel, the brighter the sky will be at the end of it. Tsumitate investors see periods of low prices as a chance to stock up for the next stage of their investment.

Lesson From Life 3: Squatting to Jump High

People mature the most after experiencing frustrations and tough times, wouldn't you agree? Each of us has experienced times when we find the strength to go on even if we just can't stop crying from all the emotional pain, or there's no end to our resentment towards someone. To overcome hardship and grow as a person, such frustrations and suffering are necessary. In both life and investing, squatting allows you to jump higher.

Chapter 4　"Increasing price" Effect:
Automatic investment vs. Lump-sum investment

All my previous examples featured falling prices. This time, I'll show you one where the price goes up. You'll see how this has a bad effect on performance compared to a lump-sum investment.

Case 5: When it doubles

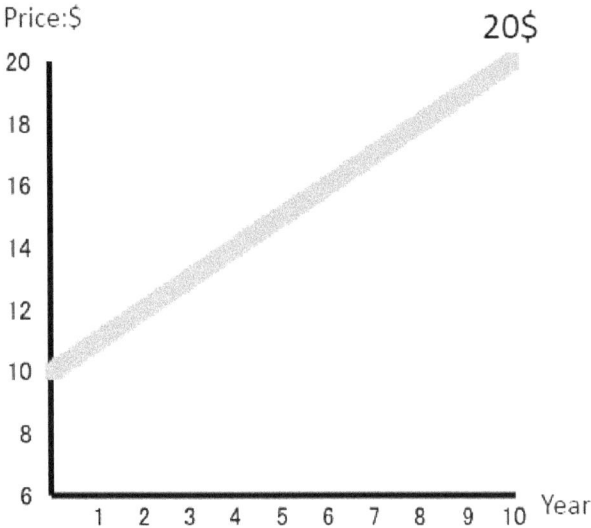

Price:$

20$

The starting price is $10 and at the 10-year mark, it doubles to $20. If tsumitate investing $100 a month in this fund, total $12,000, what would be the outcome?

1. $10,800　　2. $16,700　　3. $19,600

Which one? The answer is 2. Although you made money, it was nowhere near the $24,000 you would have gotten if you placed the $12,000 in a lump-sum at the beginning of the investment period. In this case, tsumitate investing provides less profit than lump-sum investing. What's the reason? Let's use the same formula to analyze this case.

Investment Value = Amount x Price

When tsumitate investing in a fund whose price constantly goes up, the number of units you can purchase keeps going down throughout the investment period. As a result, you buy fewer units than you would if investing a lump-sum at the start. Such a one-time, lump-sum investment in a fund whose price only goes up thereafter means you buy in at the lowest point when the highest amount of units can be purchased.

A tsumitate investment in such an ever-increasing product is not very effective compared to a lump-sum investment, but nevertheless, there is no loss. Tsumitate investing can be thought of as a source of moderate gains.

Case 6: Going up, then dipping a little

Price:$

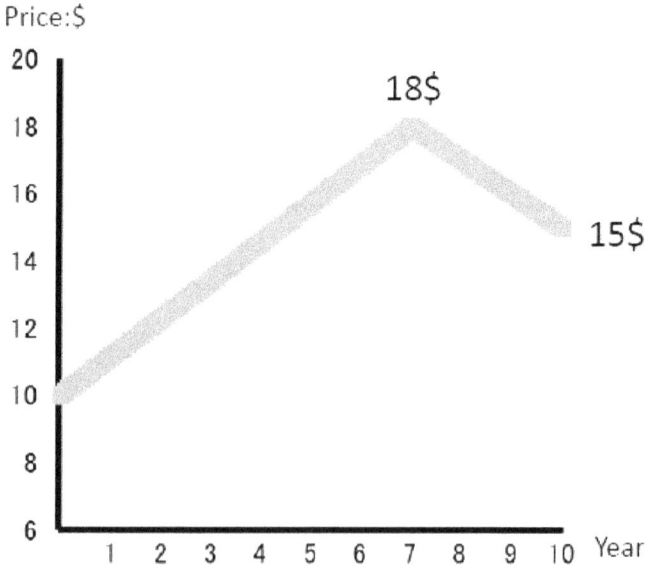

Let's look at a case where the price falls a little after a steady rise. Started at $10, it went up to $18 by the 7-year mark, then dipped to $15 after 10 years, a 50% increase from the beginning. Tsumitate investing $100 per month, $12,000 total, in this fund over 10 years would have provided how much of a return?

1. $10,200   2. $12,700   3. $14,800

What do you think? The answer is 2. Even when the fund increases by 50%, the tsumitate investor only gets a 5% profit, or $600. The reason can be understood, as you can guess, using the formula. In the end, the rising value results in a low amount of units purchased.

Case 7: Return to original price

Price:$

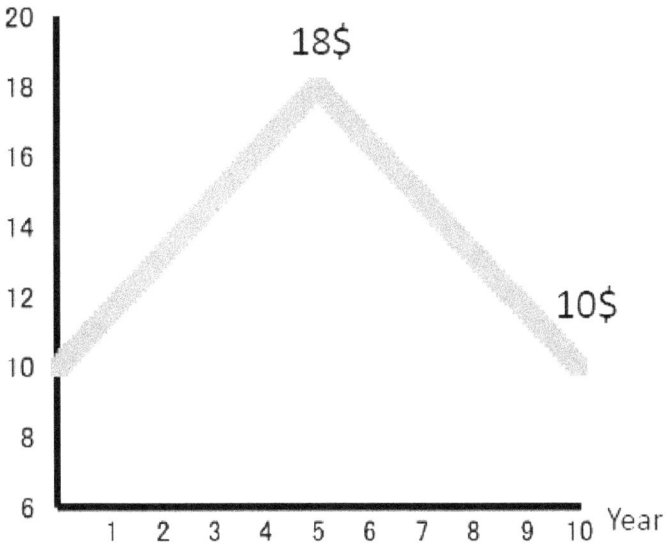

Before concluding this Chapter, let's look at one more case. Starting at $10, the fund rose to $18 after 5 years and went back down to $10 at the end of the 10-year investment period. It went up, then back down to the original price. What would be the result of a tsumitate investment of $100 monthly totaling $12,000 over the 10 years?

1. $5,940   2. $8,820   3. $10,200

What do you think? The answer is 2, unfortunately the investor is in the red. This case of a tsumitate investment that goes up and down results in a sharp decline in value. Please keep this case in mind. You carefully invest your hard-earned money only to see it washed away in the end.

It's very important to view this type of investment the right way. As I explained a little earlier, when prices fall, the amount you buy up is high. For this case, the very end of the investment period is the right time to buy lot of units.

This pattern would certainly provide negative results, but if you decide to continue, who knows what might come of this investment. That's because when prices are falling, more units can be purchased. If ending at the 10-year mark, then there would have to be some upward movement when time is up, but if continuing the tsumitate investment beyond the 10 years, that point may have some merits.

Lesson From Life 4: Good Balance is Crucial

One guy is rich but has a bad personality, while another guy is poor but has a great personality. Which one would you rather live with? This is a very difficult question. In all things, balance is important. Tsumitate investing is the same. You don't make money just from rising prices. There needs to be a balance between amount and price.

Chapter 5 "No timing" Effect: Don't worry about when to start

Many people probably worry about the best time to start investing. But with tsumitate investing, you don't have to.

Case 8: When should I start?

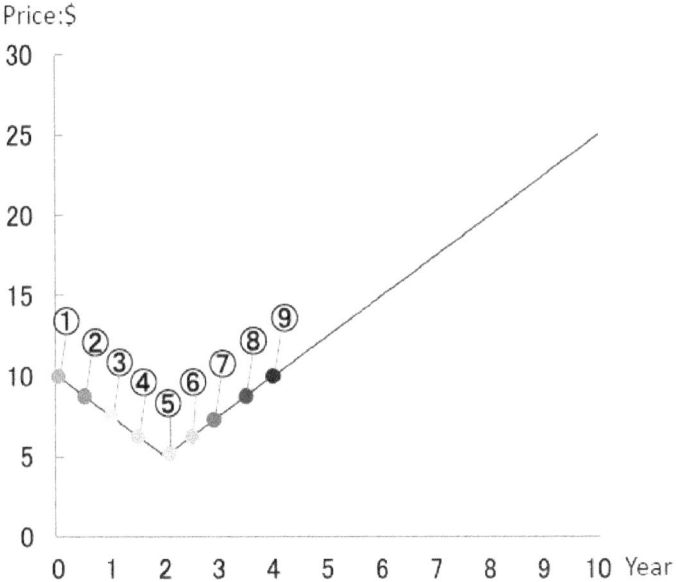

Consider a financial instrument with a price fluctuation as shown in the graph above. Although its movement over a period of only 10 years is represented, it continued to go up much the same way beyond that point. If a tsumitate investment over those 10 years was made and the numbers on the line represent start-up time options at 6-month intervals, at which point do you know you should have started to get the most out of your investment?

What do you think? The answer is 2. As a reference, the order from most to least lucrative start point is 2,3,1,4,5,6,7,8,9. You see that performance varies depending on the start-up timing. Changing the starting point would simultaneously change the amount of units you can purchase as well as the price. Ultimately, the value of the investment is decided by the result of "amount x price," so both of these factors are essential.

When you invest, you would probably consider starting at a low point, right? If making a one-time, lump-sum investment, the start-up timing is very important because the outcome depends solely on the price with the number of units staying exactly the same. (Formula: Investment Value = Amount x Price)

But this is not the case for tsumitate investing. There is no need to fuss with starting time. Why do I know this? Think for a moment. With tsumitate investing, when you start is only one of multiple times when units are purchased. A tsumitate investment spanning 10 years would provide 12 unit purchasing opportunities per year, 120 times in total. The start of the investment is but one of 120 buying times, so it has a very small effect on the overall results of the investment.

Case 9: When should I start?(2)

Price:$

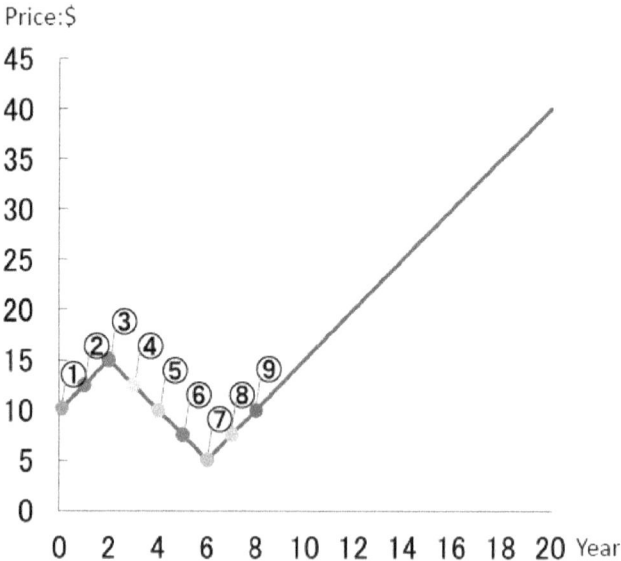

Let's solve the next problem. This time, the start-up time options are spread out at 1-year intervals for each tsumitate investment of 10 years. Of the 9 points on the line, which one should you start from to get the most out of your investment?

What do you think? The answer is 6. Although the best time to start for the previous Case was the second highest point, in this Case the best starting point is almost at the bottom. As a reference, the order from most to least would be 6,5,4,7,3,8,2,9,1. A very random order indeed. Any forecasting would be very difficult based on such data.

As you saw in the two previous cases, with tsumitate investing, starting at the lowest price doesn't necessarily provide favorable results and starting at a high price won't guarantee anything either. In the final analysis, results vary because the number of units of a fund we can purchase depends solely on how the price fluctuates after starting. The best timing is only revealed retroactively.

The time you start investing is but a single timing among multiple purchasing opportunities. So there's no point worrying about it. The best thing to do is starting early and buying as many units as possible. Tsumitate investing provides the best results when starting as soon as possible.

Accumulate

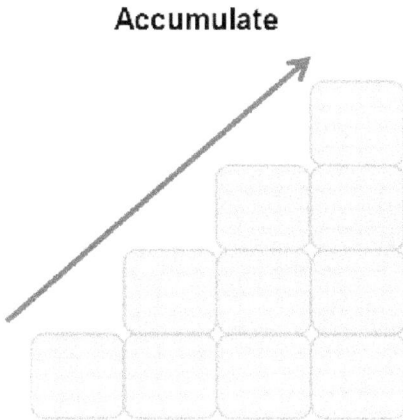

Lesson From Life 5: Act Without Fear

Any challenge in life will come with uncertainties. But after starting, many people are surprised on how easy it is.
The same applies to tsumitate investing. Even if you ponder on the best time to start, the answer will never be revealed to you. The best thing to do is act first. It's important to start tsumitate investing through plans such as 401Ks and IRAs.

Chapter 6 "Ending" Effect:
Knowing when to stop is extremely important

With tsumitate investing, although you never need to bother with the best time to start, when to stop is extremely important.

Case 10: Knowing when to stop is important

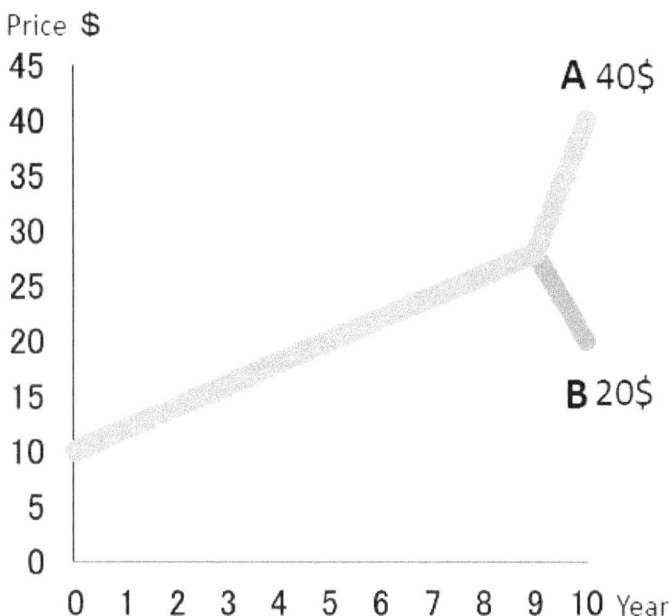

Price $

45   **A** 40$
40
35
30
25
20
15   **B** 20$
10
5
0

0   1   2   3   4   5   6   7   8   9   10   Year

The above graph shows two mutual funds that start at $10. Although they both behave the exact same way over 9 years, they move very differently the last year. Fund A increases over the final year to $40, but Fund B drops to $20 at the end. Excluding the last year, the process is almost the same. If investing $100 in each of these funds every month, what would happen to the $12,000 total investment after 10 years? Which of the following combination of results do you think were provided by these funds?

1. A: $46,874   B: $20,632
2. A: $57,378   B: $18,254
3. A: $36,019   B: $15,005
4. A: $26,288   B: $13,415

What do you think? The answer is 4. As you can see, there is an enormous gap between A and B.

In this case, they were acting almost the same over 9 years. In other words, the number of units purchased are almost the same, 657 for A and 671 for B. However, the final price is different. Fund A's $40 price at the 10-year mark is twice the $20 price of B. In the end, Fund A's earnings rate was 119.1%, whereas B's was only 11.8%. With only the final price different between them, one is twice the value of the other. The reason for this can be understood using our formula again:

Investment Value = Amount x Price

In tsumitate investing, the value of the entire lot of units accumulated over the investment period is greatly affected by the final price. The time you start is but one factor that determines a single amount of units you purchase, but your timing at the end of such an investment carries a lot more weight. Because all of the units you purchased up to the end of the investment period are affected by this final price, it has an immense impact on the performance of your investment.

As you can see from this case, the ultimate price is extremely important in tsumitate investing. That's why your exit strategy is paramount over all other concerns. After having invested over and over again all this time only to have a huge drop in the market bringing your investment value way down is a very frustrating thing. To avoid a worse case scenario, whenever a dangerous movement in the market nears, it's time to re-balance your investment to a more stable asset allocation. This theme has many features that I would rather explain in more detail separately.

To conclude this Chapter, I'd just like to ask you to please remember not to worry about when to start and focus, rather, on the all-important final price.

Lesson From Life 6: If the end result is good, it was all worthwhile

Time flies. And every human being on earth will face death sooner or later. No matter how wonderful a time you had when you were young, you will not want to end your days sad and alone.

It's the same with tsumitate investing. No matter how large the amount you purchase, a low price at the end will leave you quite unhappy. You want to see this long investment period end with a smile, don't you?

Chapter 7 "Process" Effect:
It is important to watch prices in the process, as well as those at the start and end.

With tsumitate investing, we know that where the price level ultimately stops at the end of the investment period is essential. However, how the fund behaves or moves along the way is almost equally essential. I'll show you why the process is so important.

Case 11: Even if the goal is the same

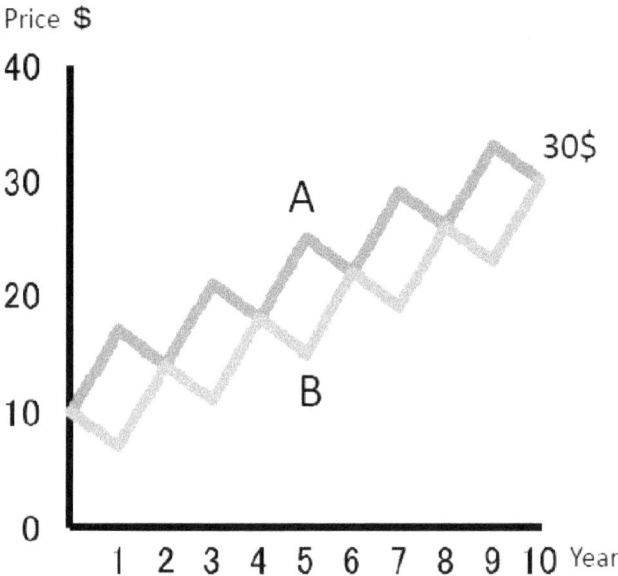

The figure has two investment funds starting at $10 per unit and ending at $30 at the 10-year mark. Although their start and end prices are the same, their movements in between vary. Fund A zigzags up then down repeatedly on an upward slope, while Fund B zigzags down then up over and over also moving upward.

If tsumitate investing in both A and B, which one will provide the most profit? A or B?

What do you think? The correct answer is B. Although they both have identical start and end prices, their final end results differ incredibly. Fund A ended with $17,420, a 45% increase, while B finished at $23,744, up 98%! Why are these investment values so disparate even after starting and ending at exactly the same place?

The reason is the amount purchased. Since the investment value is "amount" multiplied by "price," even with the same ending price, the more units are in the coffer at the end, the higher the investment value. It's simple arithmetic!

Comparing their movements, because Fund B spent more time decreasing, a greater amount of units could be purchased. With tsumitate investing, not only the final price but also its path along the way is important. This feature is hugely different from a one-time, lump-sum investment whose performance only depends on the start and end price.

Case 12: The process is important

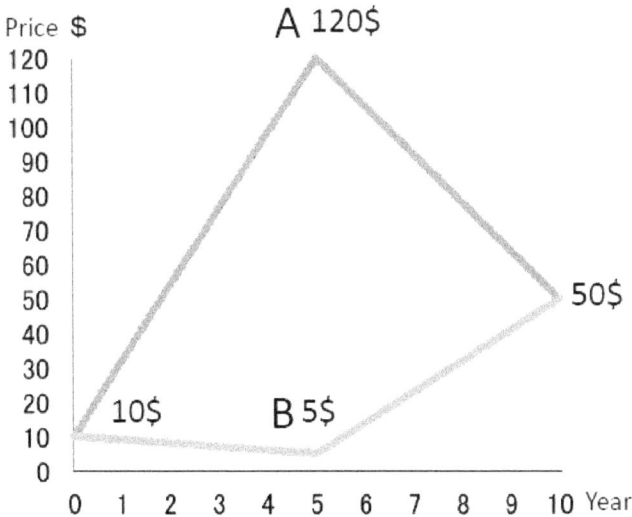

Price $

A 120$

50$

10$

B 5$

Year

Let's do one more just to train our minds. Here, both Funds A and B start off at $10 and climb all the way up to $50 at the end. Of the following combination of figures representing the end result of a tsumitate investment of $100 per month in these funds, which one is correct?

1. A: $15,314   B: $47,556
2. A: $12,225   B: $68,620
3. A: $12,225   B: $48,547
4. A: $10,737   B: $57,153

What do you think happened in this case? The answer is 4. Huge difference, isn't it? Although both funds' starting and ending prices are the same, their paths are completely different. That's why their results are different. Even though A had a 500% increase in price, it's investment value ended up in the red by about 10%, whereas B provided a profit of about 380% with the same 500% increase in price.

As I'm showing to you here, the daily movement of the price is important in tsumitate investing. Just remember that it's all about the "amount."

Lesson From Life 7: Results or Process

What's most important in life, "Results" or "Process"? In work as in life, results take precedence over everything else. But if you chase only results, there might be times when you miss out on important things. It's the same with tsumitate investing. Of course, the final price matters, but the process is also as important.

Chapter 8 "Continuity" Effect: Quitters never win

With tsumitate investing, to keep going is important. Although timing is important with lump-sum investing, it is rather the term that is important with tsumitate investing. Endurance really makes you stronger.

Case 13: If periods vary

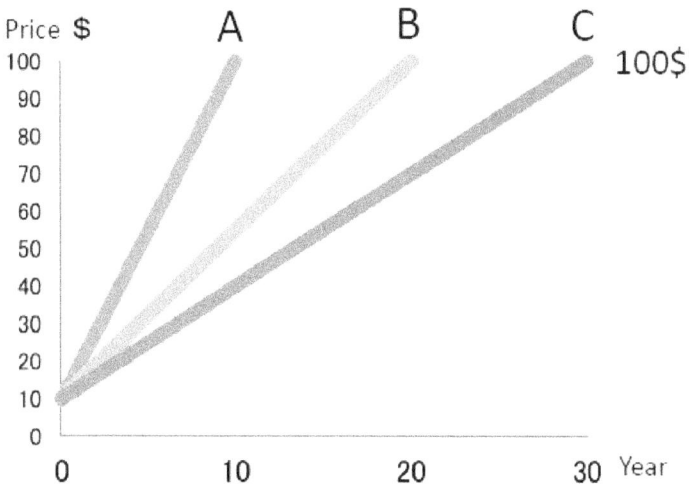

Look at the three financial instruments A, B and C. They all started at $10 and ended at $100 only A did it in only 10 years, while B took 20 years and C spanned 30 years. If having tsumitate invested $100 per month in each of these products, which one ended with the highest investment value?

This one is easy, right? Of course, C provides the most profit in the end because the longer you invest, the greater the amount of units you buy. Actual results show that Fund A ended at $31,157 ($12,000 invested; 925.6 units purchased), Fund B at $61,855

($24,000 invested; 618.6 units purchased) and Fund C at $92,555 ($36,000 invested; 311.6 units purchased).

  This is a simple but extremely important point. The key to getting great results out of tsumitate investing is to never quit. I'll explain more about this later but you won't get such fantastic results just with a high price. It's important to stay in for as long as possible always increasing the amount of units. This method of investment gives you good results as long as you stick to it.

  Although timing is most important in lump-sum investing, where success is measured by the price you bought in for, tsumitate investing centers on the term of the investment. I explained before, that you shouldn't worry about timing when tsumitate investing and its essential to start early and keep going as long as possible.

Key factor

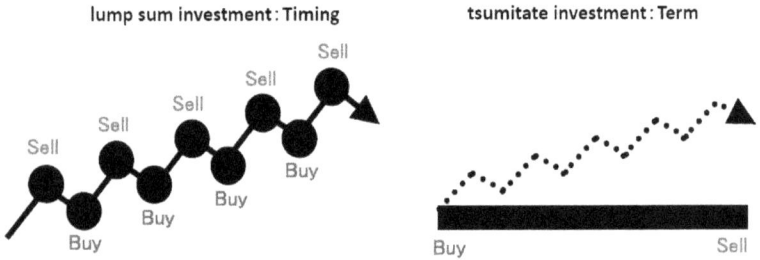

lump sum investment : Timing

tsumitate investment : Term

Lesson From Life 8: Endurance Makes You Stronger

  It is not necessary to explain about the endurance. Continuous endurance hones your skills. Tsumitate investing is the same. Continuous purchasing means higher amounts, which leads to good results.

Chapter 9 "Slow increase" Effect: Slow, rather than rapid, increases

With tsumitate investing, it's better to have a slow upward trend rather than a rapid upsurge.

Case 14: Slow increases

Price $

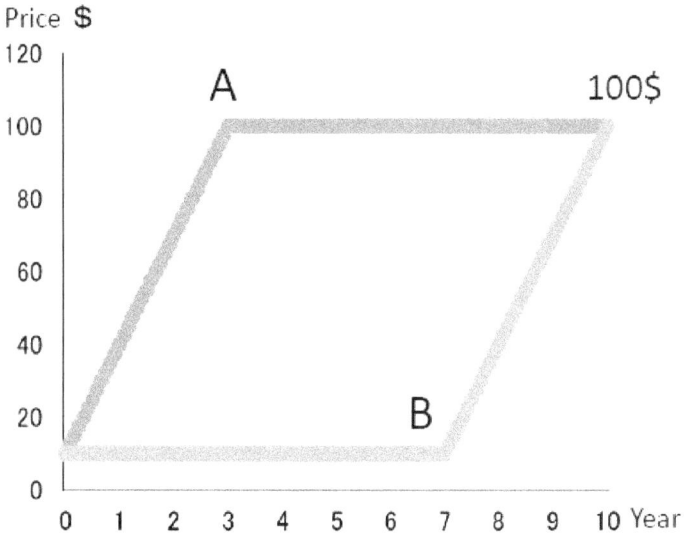

The above shows two funds A and B that both start at $10 and grow to $100. Fund A jumps sharply to $100 in 3 years then levels off, while B is flat for the first 7 years then shoots up during the last 3. If tsumitate investing $100 per month over the investment period, how will these funds perform? What is the correct combination of results?

1. A: $42,445   B: $51,276
2. A: $35,614   B: $61,852
3. A: $22,009   B: $78,208
4. A: $18,081   B: $93,681

What do you think? The correct answer is 4. With tsumitate investing, remember that the final price is important, but the price movements throughout the investment period which determines the number of units you ultimately buy is also important. In this case, even though they both reach the same point in the end, it's better to increase slowly towards that high final price in order to purchase as many units as possible and ensure a fantastic profit.

Case 15: What if it jumps 100 fold?

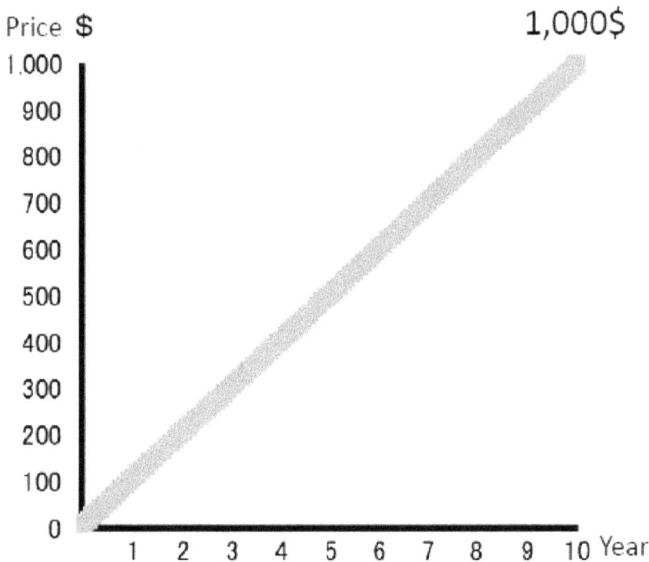

Although these cases are not real, they help you understand the features of tsumitate investing. Let's look at a special fund that grows 100 fold in 10 years from $10 to $1000. If you had invested $12,000 in a lump sum at the start of the investment period, you would have a whopping $1.2 million at the end. What would result from a tsumitate investment of $100 per month in this fund?

1. $61,400   2. $289,000   3. $632,000

What's your guess? The correct answer is 1. You must be disappointed! As you can see, even with the fund skyrocketing to 100 times its original value, a tsumitate investment only provided a 5-fold increase of your total investment.

You can understand the reason for this using our formula: Investment Value = Amount x Price. Tsumitate investing is different from any other type of investment activity, and its profits do not necessarily result from price increases. It's the amount, or the number of units, of a fund purchased and the final price that decide the fate of your investment.

With tsumitate investing, you have to change your focus from "products with increasing prices" to "products that let you stock up on units."

One of the biggest differences between tsumitate investing and one-time, lump-sum investing is the motivation of the investor. Tsumitate investments are not effective when prices shoot up quickly, but rather provide more satisfaction when prices increase slowly over the long term. Contrastingly, lump-sum investing works better when prices go up quickly rather than slowly.

To put it in other words, lump-sum investments motivate you by making you wish for short-term spikes, while tsumitate investments are for those betting on slow, long-term increases. These two kinds of investments provide two completely contrary motivations.

lump sum investment

More effective with short-term price increases

Price

time

tsumitate investment

More effective with long-term price increases

Price

time

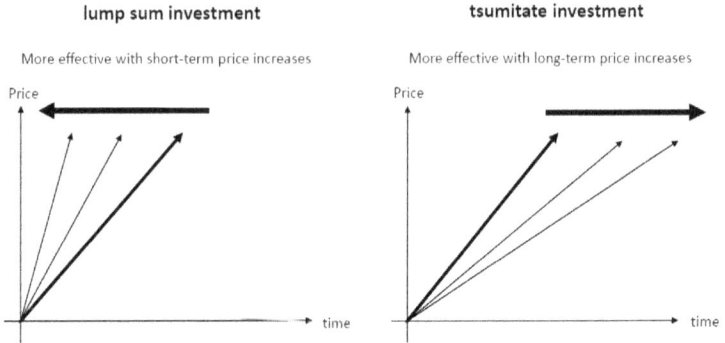

Many people believe that good investments involve buying low and selling high. This is not the case for tsumitate investing. Results are not determined simply by the starting and finishing prices. It's the number of units you stock up during the entire process that counts in the end.

This booklet gave me a chance to share with the world this new investment concept of focusing on "amount" as much as "price."

Lesson From Life 9: Sometimes Slower is Better

With work, speed is always demanded of you. But when spending time with family, it's best to go slow and savor every moment. It's the same with investing. Some investments provide returns from rapidly increasing prices, however, tsumitate investing is more effective with funds that go up slowly. Some investments are like that.

Chapter 10 "No predicting" Effect: I don't remember putting any thought into it

It's very difficult to make precise forecasts with tsumitate investing, and such forecasts are futile. I'll explain next why forecasting with tsumitate investing is unnecessary.

Case 16: Vertically symmetric

Price: $

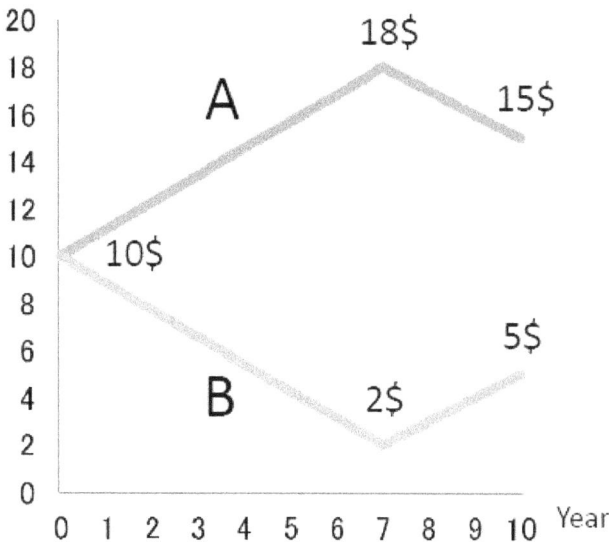

The above shows the movements of two funds A and B which are vertically symmetrical to each other starting at $10. Fund A goes up to $18 after 7 years, then falls finishing at $15 after 10 years. On the other hand, B sinks to $2 at the 7-year mark, and then turns up finishing at $5 after 10 years. As mutual funds, A is clearly the better performer. But which one would prevail under a tsumitate investment?

This one is easy, right? The answer is B. Although A's final price is much higher, that fund didn't allow the investor to purchase as many units. I've said over and over again in this booklet that a tsumitate investment's performance does not only depend on price.

Those of you who have read the entire booklet up to this point will have understood this, but please think carefully for a moment. If I had shown you this graph at the very beginning before any explanation, you would have automatically picked Fund A, right?

If you looked at this graph and picked B as obviously the better fund for tsumitate investing, you have graduated into the proud class of elite tsumitate investors!

Case 17: 8 zigzag funds3

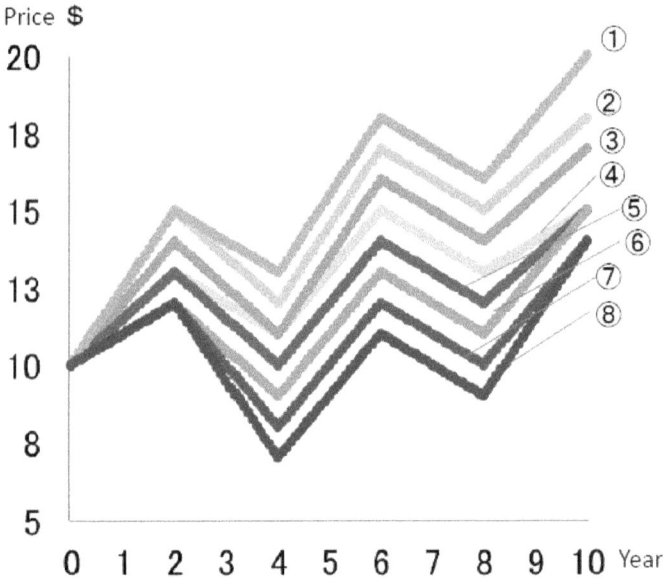

The graph shows 8 funds with similar fluctuations over the investment period. If tsumitate investing in each of these funds, which one would give you the highest profit?

What do you think? The answer is 8. I'm sure most of you got it right. This proves that you're aware of the need to buy lots of units to succeed in tsumitate investing.

Case 18: Another 8 zigzag funds

Well then, which one do you think came in second? This is the last problem we will solve. In fact, being able to figure out the No. 2 fund in this graph is the most important point of this case. So which one is it?
I'm sure many of you think 6 came in second. Most people I've encountered in my career chose 6, but the right answer is 1, the fund that increases the most throughout the investment period.

Please remember our formula: Investment Value = Amount x Price

When valuating an investment, the amount is certainly very important. But equally as important is the final price. One is not more important than the other. A good balance of these two factors determines the result of your investment.
In this case, Fund 8 accumulated the most units so it provided the best results. Fund 1's final price was the highest so it came in second. Success here was determined by a balance between amount and price and was very difficult to guess.

Just for your reference, the order of funds from best to worst is 8,1,6,7,3,2,5,4. I'm sure no one was able to guess that. As you can see, fund performance is totally random.

Next, let's take a look at the ranking of the funds at the 9th year mark. The order from best to worst for that year is 1,8,2,3,6,7,5,4. You can see that this order is completely different from the last one.

This is why forecasting the performance of tsumitate investments is extremely difficult. What's important is to invest in products that will increase in the future. Predicting other things like minor movements during the investment period is totally unnecessary.

In the world of investing, financial institutions are putting a great deal of effort into giving their products even a slightly high performance. However, the moment tsumitate investing is involved, the performance of the fund and the results of the investment become separate factors. In the world of tsumitate investing, success does not only come from the best performing funds. This is perhaps a bit ironic, but it's the truth.

With tsumitate investing, winning or losing with respect to the market is meaningless. Rather, you simply ride the wave of price fluctuations like a surfer. A very energy-saving way of investing. No need to worry about picking just the right product. Tsumitate investing has been well-known for many years, however, its features have never been clearly revealed.

Lesson From Life 10: Act Without Worry

Some people worry all the time. If some decision could come of it, then it wouldn't have been in vain, but most of the time it was all for nothing. Don't you agree? If thinking doesn't provide results, then you should act first. That's when you'll notice something you didn't before, or meet that new someone, or learn something new. This is also true for tsumitate investing, where it's important to act without worry and keep going.

Chapter 11 Conclusion:
What is tsumitate investing?

So what exactly is tsumitate investing? Let's summarize all the features I've talked about in this booklet.

List of tsumitate investing effects

1	"Relief from falling prices" Effect	No matter how low the price falls
2	"Speedy recovery" Effect	Rapid recovery from losses
3	"Rebound" Effect	Gain returns if bouncing back after a drop
4	"Increasing price" Effect	Automatic investment < Lump-sum investment
5	"No timing" Effect	Don't worry about when to start
6	"Ending" Effect	Knowing when to stop is extremely important
7	"Process" Effect	It is important to watch prices in the process, as well as those at the start and end.
8	"Continuity" Effect	Quitters never win
9	"Slow increase" Effect	Slow, rather than rapid, increases
10	"No predicting" Effect	I don't remember putting any thought into it

This list contains several psychological effects such as "relief from falling prices," "recovery from losses," "no timing" and "no predicting" as well as familiar values such as "continuity."

These are all psychological effects that serve to relieve the stress associated with investing. I believe that this unquantifiable "peace of mind" can only be found in tsumitate investing.

Up to now, the value and measure of lump-sum investments have been represented in quantifiable terms such as "profit," "yield," "investment efficiency," "cost" and "risk." These are all quantitative values expressed on the number line.

If you always chase "quantitative values," you may increase the risk of losses. Risk and returns is a tradeoff. The world of investing shows us that Low Risk = Low Return = Low Stress, and High Risk = High Return = High Stress.

On the other hand, tsumitate investing described in this booklet is not necessarily a highly efficient means compared with lump-sum investing. This was demonstrated with a fund that increased

100 times but only provided a profit of 5 times the total value of the tsumitate investment. Definitely it's not going to make you a fortune.

As a tradeoff, it provides peace of mind thanks to its "rapid recovery from losses." In an investment climate where market crashes occur every few years, the "resilience" of tsumitate investing is a feature of paramount importance to investors. It's a "Medium Risk = Medium Return = No Stress" investment method.

Tsumitate investing is in no way universal. It has good aspects and bad ones. What's important is to understand its features and formulate an investment strategy that fits your life plan. Please try to view it as one of your investment choices. I would be thrilled if this booklet helps you manage your investments.

Differences In lump Sum Investment And Tsumitate Investment

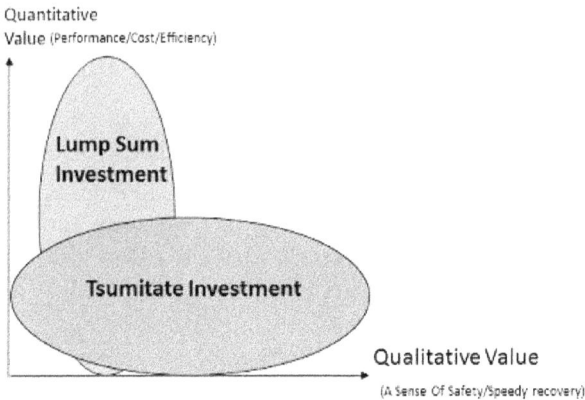

Quantitative
Value (Performance/Cost/Efficiency)

Lump Sum Investment

Tsumitate Investment

Qualitative Value
(A Sense Of Safety/Speedy recovery)

Conclusion

As a member of the financial industry, I wanted to contribute to the asset formation of as many people as possible. Even if I could reach only one person, it would have been worthwhile. So for many years, I enthusiastically researched all there was to know about tsumitate investing. It was an extremely somber and lonesome endeavor that no one before me has ever attempted.

The more I researched, the more I became aware of the appeal of tsumitate investing. I constantly uncovered new features that needed to be unraveled. At some point, I became enchanted with this research.

I then told my colleagues, friends and acquaintances all about the wonders of tsumitate investing. "Wow! That's interesting!," "I had no idea!" ...many of them seemed very happy to hear about it. I had so much fun that, even though I made very little money, I totally immersed myself in it. Even after my company was sold and I became independent, I still continued the research. Then, I published a book under one of the largest publishing companies in Japan. The public reaction was more than I ever expected, as over 70 reviews of my book were made by bloggers. I received support from many luminaries of Japan's financial industry which led to this release in English.

My solemn wish is to change the image of investing for all people. I want to eradicate the fear of investing many have. To do this, I want to share the features of tsumitate investing with the world.

For all those who feel as I do, all the graphs presented in this booklet are available free of charge on my website. Download them and use them to teach your family members, partners, colleagues, friends and acquaintances that with tsumitate investing there is nothing to fear when prices fall. They'll all think you care so much for them. I want you to experience the same joy I felt when I was doing this research.

With all the advancements in medicine, our life expectancy is increasing with every passing generation. No matter where you live, you cannot depend on the government to support you. Each of us will have to build our own future assets and tsumitate investing is the most effective means for the ordinary person to achieve this.

Let's spread the word about tsumitate investing. Let's change the image that investing has in the world. It is not a scary thing.

Let's eradicate the notion that people lose money when prices go down and build a new conventional wisdom about investing.

Many people across the globe cannot invest even if they want to. But let's teach them about the importance of accumulating for the future. This is the duty of all of us fortunate enough to be born in rich countries. From today forward, you take the lead. Let's bring the message out together. I dream of the day when "tsumitate" becomes a household word.

Mr.Tsumitate
Yasuhira Hoshino

Appendix A: Messages from Japanese Financial Sector

**1. Kazuhisa Okamoto : CFA(Chartered Financial Analyst)
Founder, Chief Executive and Representative Director
I-O Wealth Advisors, Inc.**

**2.Atsuto Sawakami : Representative Director & CEO,
Sawakami Asset Management Inc.**

**3.Satoshi Nojiri : Head of Fidelity Investor Education
Institute**

**4.Ken Shibusawa : Founder & Chairman, Commons Asset
Management**

5.Hideto Fujino: Founder, Director, Chief Investment Officer, RHEOS CAPITAL WORKS Inc.

6.Koichi Ito : Certified Tax Accountant, CFP, Professor of the Graduate School of Accounting and Finance of Chiba University of Commerce

7.Yasuyuki Kamata : President of Kamakura Investment Management Co., Ltd.

8.Akinori Kamiji : Visiting Professor at the Institute of Innovation Management (finance) of the Graduate School of Shinshu University

9.Shinji Kimura : CFA(Chartered Financial Analyst)

10.Anonymous: financial media person ①

11.Anonymous: financial media person ②

1. Kazuhisa Okamoto: CFA(Chartered Financial Analyst) Founder, Chief Executive and Representative Director I-O Wealth Advisors, Inc.

I guess that many people will recognize the power of the method by reading this book.

What's been explained in this book should be something "needless to say." But, in the real world, this is forgotten and may come as a surprise to many of the readers, especially to those who have little experience in investing.

"Aging population" is becoming a serious problem in many advanced nations. Japan is the forerunner of the trend. The environment of the Japanese economy and society has completely changed in the last 20 years, and there has been growing concern about the future, especially among young people.

They are often told "it is only you, not anyone else, who would take care of your future life." People say "Therefore, you have to take risks to accumulate your assets". However, they often hear the stories of people who had terrible experiences in the markets. So, they are at a loss what to do.

Risk-taking is different from doing something dangerous. Taking risks rationally is crucial for long term investing. One aspect of the basics, the effect of dollar cost averaging, is the focus of the book written by Mr. Yasuhira Hoshino.

In the book, the author describes in detail the effects of TSUMITATE INVESTMENT, a Japanese term for Dollar Cost Averaging Method. I guess that many people will recognize the power of the method by reading this book. To sum up, in life-long asset formation, the longer the protracted bear markets, the more you can accumulate financial assets at lower prices. Thus, as a result, when it's time to finally use the funds, they will be profitable even with a little rise. The book gives this valuable realization to its readers.

The idea introduced in the book provide investors with endurance against short-term market fluctuations, in this sense, I think the book has a significant meaning.

Let me say a few words about the future agenda. The condition for this technique to be effective is that stock prices will rise in the end. In Japan, the stock price level is about one-quarter of the peak recorded more than 20 years ago. With TSUMITATE INVESTMENT to materialize its strength, in the end, "what do you own" is the vital question. I hope the author will eventually provide the answer to this important question.

Having said that, I believe the book is an excellent introduction to life-long investing and I hope many people start accumulation of financial assets for their post retirement life. Any good idea without accompanying action has no meaning.

Profile

Kazuhisa Okamoto
Kaz Okamoto, CFA(Chartered Financial Analyst)
Founder, Chief Executive and Representative Director
I-O Wealth Advisors, Inc.
Chairman Emeritus, CFA Society of Japan

Having spent 13 years since inception in the position of Chief Executive-Japan of Barclays Global Investors Japan Limited (BGI), Kaz Okamoto has started his own firm, I-O Wealth Advisors, Inc. in May 2005. The firm is engaged in providing seminars on life-long wealth and asset management for middle class private investors. Prior to joining BGI in 1992, He served as director of Institutional Sales and Research for Nikko International in New York, Chief Analyst and Strategist for Nikko Securities and General Manager of Quantitative Portfolio Management for Nikko International Capital Management.

He is the author of many books, including Long-term Investing up to the Age of 100, Investing by Teachings of Lao-Tzu and Chuang-Tzu, Money Lessons for a Family, Asset Formation – A Japanese Way. He received a BA in Economics from Keio University and earned his Chartered Financial Analyst (CFA) designation in 1983. He served as vice chairman and director of Japan Securities Investment Advisors Association in 2000/2002, a board member of Investment Trust Association of Japan in 2004/2005, and Chairman of CFA Society of Japan (2004-2006, currently Chairman Emeritus). He is a member of the Japan Association of Corporate Executives (Keizai Doyukai). http://www.i-owa.com/

2. Atsuto Sawakami:Representative Director & CEO, Sawakami Asset Management Inc.

The uniquness of this book is that it analyzes the strong points of dollar-cost-average investment by presenting many investment models.

This book is likely to stir an interesting concern among investors, not only individuals but also institutional investors.

Dollar cost average investment is not a brand new idea. Many investors are actually practicing it. However, the uniqueness of this book is that it analyzes the strong points of the dollar-cost-average investments by presenting many investment models. Reading this book, individual investors may get more assured with the money stock purchasing policy regardless the market fluctuation.

At the mutual fund industry, this book will remind the importance of Dollar cost average investment in their marketing. After the Financial Babble burst, quite a many subscribers rushed to liquidate their stock investment position, and therefore the mutual fund industry has encountered sizable repurchase orders. Facing to the substantial stock market crash, it is really hard to persuade individuals and household to become positive to buy stock investment.

That is why this book can be of big support to the mutual fund marketing. Stock market is not yet boiled in the US, it is an ideal timing to put the Dollar cost average investment method into practice. Earlier start of monthly stock purchasing practice, individuals may get larger number of shares at weak market, which will help investors make fortune.

In Japan, we are managing investment trust fund of US$2.8 billion over 120,000 subscribers at present. Nearly half of subscribers have contracts with us to buy our fund every month. This helps a lot of our portfolio management. Due to this service with subscription, we are enjoying net money inflow for 135 months in low since inception. Thanks to the constant inflow of new money, we could buy Japanese stocks massively at any market crash such as the Subprime problem, the Leman Shock, and the Greece Crisis. Our fund itself has been making Dollar cost average investment, and consequently, we are always far ahead of the Japanese stock index.

I believe this book describe both the benefit and the limitation of this investment philosophy very well in detail. There are many books written regarding investments. However, I believe this book is very unique in the point that it is truly focusing on the needs of financial consumers.

Profile

Atsuto Sawakami
CEO of Sawakami Asset Management Inc.
Representative of Sawakami LLC
Mr. Sawakami started his career in the field of investment business as an analyst and fund advisor at Capital International in Switzerland starting 1970. Later on, he was posted as the Representative of Pictet & Cie Japan from 1980 to 1996. Subsequently he established an independent asset advisory management company, Sawakami Asset Management

Inc.(SAMI) which offered investment advisory services to its clients, based on the long-term views.

Three years later, in 1999, SAMI embarked the Sawakami Fund, an open-ended fund starting with a mere initial investment asset of 1.6 billion yen. As of Sep 1st. 2008, the fund's assets has amounted to over 200 billion yen with 110 thousand plus fund holders in nine years since its inception. AUM growth was achieved through word-of-mouth communication among the fund holders as SAMI doesn't leverage any traditional marketing communications such as CM, DM or tele-marketing and so on. SAMI is dedicated to direct-marketing and places overall clients' interests side-by-side with its long-term investment policies. In fact, SAMI will always hold on to its long-term investment policy as Mr. Sawakami's mission is to make the long-term investment a more common choice for the asset building of Japanese households.

1947 Born in Nagoya, Aichi Pref., Japan 1970 – 74 Analyst and fund advisor at Capital International in Switzerland

1973 Studied at the Graduate Institute of International Studies, Geneva

1979 – 96 Representative of Pictet & Cie Japan

1996 Established Sawakami Asset Management Inc.

1999 Inception of the "Sawakami Fund", the first publicly-offered investment trust managed by a stand-alone (non-affiliated) asset management company

http://www.sawakami.co.jp/english/

3. Satoshi Nojiri: Head of Fidelity Investor Education Institute

The aspect which has not been discussed in the past is explained.

In Japan, which has become a super aged society unprecedented in the world, baby boomers who will be joining groups of 65 or over in age in 2012 and the following generations are burdened by significant challenges. While the current younger groups in their 20s and 30s are responsible for supporting large numbers of senior citizens under the national pension system and universal health care system, these young people cannot expect same support as those current senior citizens have when they become elderly. In that sense, they are in the generation of dual burdens: they support senior citizens, while they must proceed with preparation of their own retirement income. For these younger generation, the biggest and the only weapon in asset management is 'time'. Dollar Cost Averaging Method is the way which allows us to utilize the "time" for our preparation of retirement income.

The author takes up the subject of the Dollar Cost Averaging Method and tries to explain its special features to individual investors clearly. However, the biggest characteristic of the book is that the author tries to describe the Dollar Cost Averaging Method as the progressive approach to the investment rather than the defensive aspect that it is just'bringing down the average unit price'. In the words of the author, Dollar Cost Averaging Method is an investment strategy for Individual Investors in order not to lose money. Also, from the perspective of behavioral economics which is getting attention recently, the method like Dollar Cost Averaging which is ruling out the behavioral bias is one of the strategies to provide shortcuts to more success in investment for individual investors. As such, the book offers understandable and more practical contents.

Profile

Satoshi Nojiri
Head of Fidelity Investor Education Institute

Several experiences in the research departments of Japanese and overseas securities firms as research analyst, research marketing and an advisor for individual investors.
Graduated from Hitotsubashi University.
A member of the Securities Analysts Association of Japan, the Society of the Economic Studies of Securities, the Japan Society of Household Economics, Japan Academic Society for Financial Planning and the Association of Behavioral Economics and Finance.
Wrote many books.
http://www.fidelity.co.jp/retirement/index.html

4. Ken Shibusawa:Founder & Chairman, Commons Asset Management

Mr.Hoshino has invested his life in digging deeper and further into this subject than any athoer individual.

Japan has not been an easy market to make money these days. Yet, using the "Tsumitate Method," as described by Yasuhira Hoshino's new book, one does not need an upward trending market to make money. If one made a lump sum investment in the Japanese equity index at the peak of the bubble in 1990, without any chance of turning a profit, it would be presently worth about 25% of original value. However, if one made the same investment, but utilizing the "Tsumitate Method," he would have been profitable on nine occasions, during the same period.
What is this "Tsumitate Method"? American readers will know it as "dollar cost averaging." A time tasted long term investment strategy of buying a fixed amount of securities at a fixed time intervals, say monthly.
This is not rocket-science stuff. But it is solid material. And, Mr.Hoshino has invested his life in digging deeper and further

into this subject than any other individual. I was already a believer, but his book revealed merits that were truly enlightening.

In traditional investment, "trend is your friend." But if you had invested in a lump sum, a trend can be your foe, if that trend is downwards. With the "Tsumitate Method," it is "volatility" that becomes your friend. Even if the market sells off, as long one sticks to the method, he only needs to see a correction to be profitable.

Diversification of risk is not just about allocation of assets, but also allocation of time. By spreading out one's investment over the long term, it is "time" that also becomes your friend.

Why should a method that was successful in Japan be of any use, outside of the country? Well, if you think your home market will always and forever trend upwards, then the "Tsumitate Method" is of no use. However, if you think there is uncertainty ahead, and the markets may be in for a rough stretch, then "Tsumitate Method" is the way. It's no sweat.

Profile

Ken Shibusawa
Founder and Chief Executive Officer, Shibusawa and Company, Inc.
Founding Member and Chairman, Commons Asset Management
Ken Shibusawa founded Shibusawa and Company, Inc. in 2001, and Commons Asset Management, a mutual fund dedicated to deliver long term investment opportunities to the Japanese household, in 2008. He has extensive market experience at top-tier US investment banks and a premier global hedge fund.
His non-profit associations include: Shibusawa Eiichi Memorial Foundation ("Father" of Japanese capitalism), Keizai Doyukai

(Japan Association of Corporate Executives), where he is vice
chairman of the Committees of the Americas, Japan Center for
International Exchange, Healthcare Policy Institute Japan,
among others.
He is also a published author and writes frequently in magazines,
journals, and internet media.
He was educated in the United States from second grade
elementary through college (University of Texas, BS Chemical
Engineering, 1983), and then returned again for graduate school
(UCLA, MBA, 1987).
http://www.commons30.jp/

5. Hideto Fujino: Founder, Director, Chief Investment Officer, RHEOS CAPITAL WORKS Inc.

This book gives you a logical explanation of how the dollar-cost- averaged investment efficiently works.

Since April 2008, a medical check-up for some diseases due to
keep irregular hours or eat unhealthy foods such as diabetes has
been introduced in Japan. After that, people in Japan especially
office workers, commonly start taking care of their health. Some
of them get into the habit of using exercise machines or hiring a
personal coach. The others often take supplements for keep up
their health. Moreover, a science-based training is getting
common too.

It was impossible that non-athlete people using exercise
machines or taking a science-based training for improving their
health in Japan. The introduction of medical check-up has
changed the Japanese people's mind for importance of their
health.

Is this phenomenon able to be applied to the field of
investment?

The pension benefit in Japan will be smaller in terms of the decline of number of Japanese people. The Japanese seniority based pay system, which people easily get increase amount of payment is going to corrupt in the money or invest for their future, so the money flow gets stuck that can throughout the Japanese economy.

You do not require any qualification or need to meet any conditions to begin investing, in the same way as with the health topic above. People tend to think that investment is only possible with a large amount of money, and they put off the decision to start investing. However, it is necessary to invest a little at a time, particularly for those who do not have large assets. It is important to start as early as possible to enable continuous investment. Time is limited, so it is a waste of time to delay starting. We only live for a limited number of years, which means that the time we have to invest is also limited, and the number of rest of days will decrease every day. Therefore, you must utilize your time efficiently.

This book gives you a logical explanation of how the dollar-cost-averaged investment efficiently works. I hope that as many people as possible will learn about the benefits of accumulating investments through this book.

Profile

Hideto Fujino
RHEOS CAPITAL WORKS Inc. Director
Founded Rheos Capital Works in 2003 following a career at Goldman Sachs Asset Management, Jardine Fleming (currently JP Morgan Fleming Asset Management) and Nomura Asset Management. Has served as Chief Investment Officer (CIO)

since the founding. Abundant experience as a fund manager with a deep expertise in small mid cap and emerging growth equity investments.
http://www.rheos.jp/english/

6.Koichi Ito:Certified Tax Accountant, CFP, Professor of the Graduate School of Accounting and Finance of Chiba University of Commerce

ICHIRO-STYLE INVESTMENT

Just as Asia has been further incorporated into investment outlets since the Lehman shock, investment methods have also seemed to be more conscious of Asia styles. Just as Ichiro has incorporated baseball with home run image to be changed into baseball with continuous hitting image, Mr. Yasuhira Hoshino has enhanced and deepened significantly American-style Dollar Cost Averaging to be turned into Asian Ichiro-style investment method. Whatever type of pitch is thrown toward him, Ichiro continues to deliver the same style of hits with his mind 'empty'. He reminds me of a Zen monk who devotes his life in training. The Ichiro-style investment method is not to win by one's power and timing but to accept every market fluctuation and take advantage of it skillfully and steadily. The concept of Mr. Yasuhira Hoshino just looks like that in my view. This investment method should be spread not only in the US but also in Asia, shouldn't it?

Profile

Koichi Ito
Certified tax accountant, CFP
Professor of the Graduate School of Accounting and Finance of
Chiba University of Commerce Specializing in personal finance,
the theory of life design, and the theory of life planning
Discussing finance and asset management in terms of the theory
of happiness Certified tax accountant, CFP Executive Director
of the Board of Japan Association for Financial Planners
Director of the Board of Japan Academic Society for Financial
Planning A member of the Consumer Affairs Council of Saitama
Prefecture Advisor of the Counseling Office for Financial
Planning of SONY
Appeared on some TV programs such as "Seikatsu hot morning
(Everyday life Hot Morning)" and "Diagnosing Your Home
Budget" of NHK, etc. as well as wrote many articles in
newspapers, magazines, and web sites.
Working on educating financial economy. He wrote many books.
http://www.polano.jp/

7.Yasuyuki Kamata:President of Kamakura Investment Management Co., Ltd.

'Investment truth' is very simple. This book will be a new
bible to defend your assets.

I am one of those who strongly hope to globally spread the book of Mr. Yasuhira Hoshino and the culture of accumulation investment explained in the book.

Everyone dreams of succeeding in investment. Even if the markets have plunged, everyone wishes to protect at least their assets. Some people may want to obtain new financial products with possibly quick returns, even if they have to pay higher fees. On the other hand, not a few people may think that they have nothing to do with investments, as their salaries are small. I want all these people to read this book by all means.

The investment method still profitable even when the market prices drop by half, the simplest investment method applicable to all the assets anywhere in the world that can start easily with a small amount of money without the need for cumbersome future projections: that's 'TSUMITATE INVESTMENT'.

I regard the book as the world's first explanatory book that shows the effectiveness of TSUMITATE INVESTMENT from multifaceted perspectives. Needless to say, their dimensions are totally different from theories all investments textbooks have conveyed in full, that is, diversified investment, long-term investment, and the effects of compound interest. In addition, no difficult formulas are used in the book. With much use of easily understandable graphs, this book will surely be easy to read and user-friendly to individual investors.

It is certain that the acceleration of globalization and the expansion of speculative money will certainly further strengthen the degree of concurrent direction and fluctuations in capital markets. We must protect our assets from these highly uncertain markets. This book teaches us that the 'investment truth' to protect one's assets is actually very simple. I'm sure that this book will be a new bible for individual investors all over the world.

Profile

Yasuyuki Kamata
President of Kamakura Investment Management Co., Ltd.
Joined Mitsui Trust and Banking Company, Limited in April,
1988. He was in charge of fund management, portfolio
management, planning products, etc.
Joined Berkley's Global Investors Trust and Banking, Inc. in
February 1999.
Assumed positions such as director of investment management
and general manager of the client relations group controlling the
asset management and overall sales of enterprise pension and
public pension, etc.
Became the president in January 2007 and vice president in April
2007 controlling the overall sales operations.
Founded Kamakura Investment Management Co., Ltd. after he
left the company on good terms in January 2008,
http://www.kamakuraim.jp/

8.Akinori Kamiji:Visiting Professor at the Institute of Innovation Management (finance) of the Graduate School of Shinshu University

This book will give a new perspective to the world of asset management.

I do want this book to be read by not only general individual
investors but also people in financial institutions involved in
mutual funds. There are two reasons:

One reason is that banks and securities firms which are on seller side do not recommend accumulation investment to their customers strongly, even if it is an excellent management technique for individual investors. This should be because incentives to put effort into accumulation investment do not work at the expense of quick profits. I am convinced that winners who will ultimately achieve success in mutual fund business are those who can 'systematize' accumulation investment. Who will do this first? That's what interests me most right now.

It can be said that our asset management industry is a history in which highly capable personnel have accumulated researches and actual proof in order to enhance 1% APY. However, after the filter called TSUMITATE INVESTMENT, the common sense of the conventional asset management will not be the common sense any more. That is because funds with good management results do not always lead to favorable returns for TSUMITATE investors. This book will give a new perspective to the world of asset management.

Profile

Akinori Kamiji
Visiting Professor of the Institute of Innovation Management (finance) the Graduate School of Shinshu University
Graduated from the Faculty of Economics of Gakushuin University
Joined Morgan Stanley Securities
Worked as a part-time instructor of the faculty of economics of Meiji Gakuin University, and assumed the post of senior managing director of Japan Investors Securities, Co., Ltd.

Designing new social systems in various fields of the financial system, pension, welfare, and education responding to the paradigm shift of the society where the population will decrease in the coming future.

Devoted to the activities of promoting the making of independent "one's own pension system" especially without relying on the national system.

Wrote many books.

9.Shinji Kimura, CFA(Chartered Financial Analyst)

I wish many people learn about Tsumitate investment and execute it in order to achieve the creation of wealth, or real fruit of investment.

Working in the financial industry and being an investor for long time, one thing I found out from my own experience and what all the experienced investors would agree with is that when people fail in investing, most of the time, it is not caused by a market crash or an economic slowdown or any of those external factors. However, most of the time, it is caused by something inside us or human behavior. Unfortunately, human brain is not very good at making sound investment decisions continuously. After people start investing and when the value of the investment starts moving up and down, without extensive experience and investment education, people become slave of greed and fear, and become out of control. People are swayed by the random walk of the market. With greed and fear that all of us have in some extent, people could not make right investment decisions, rather they tend to make bad decisions. When people regret, they don't usually ask themselves "Why did the market crash?", or "Why did the company made loss?", but they usually ask themselves "Why did I purchase at that point?" or "Why did I sell at that point?": "Why did I" type of questions. People always regret about the unnecessary and bad investment actions they took by themselves. Those actions are actually ordered by their brains which are largely affected by greed and fear. Tumitate investment is the best way to overcome this human behavior which is easily affected by greed and fear which will then lead to a wrong decision and failure. Tsumitate investment allows all the investors to always stay calm in any market environments and succeed without great deal of experience or education. It offers people peace of mind. I wish many people learn about Tsumitate investment and execute it in order to achieve the creation of wealth, or real fruit of investment.

Profie

Shinji Kimura, CFA
Graduated from Simon Fraser University, Burnaby, Canada (BBA, concentrated in Finance and Management Science, Honors). Head of Marketing & Communications, Baring Asset Management (Japan) Limited. Before joining Barings, he worked for Nippon Investors Securities Co., Ltd. where he assumed head of Planning Department.

10.Anonymous: financial media person 1

This book should be definitely read by people working at financial institutions which handle mutual fund-related business

The reason why I want readers in the US to widely read this book comes from my hope that they recognize an extremely effective asset formation technique for individual investors, called TSUMITATE INVESTMENT. I want this book to be definitely read by people working at financial institutions which handle mutual fund-related business, as well as general individual investors.

TSUMITATE INVESTMENT is more effective in a situation like today's volatile markets. This investment method is extremely safe and superior for the asset formation of individual investors. However, the reality in Japan is that banks and securities firms, which are the sellers, are not so eager to recommend the method to individual investors, due to poor appeal of commission income. Nevertheless, amid the growing awareness of the management and asset formation among individual investors, in the wake of concerns about pension, I expect that financial institutions which understand such individual needs and can 'systematize' TSUMITATE INVESTMENT as shown in the book will be the winners in the 21st century. This is what interests the author and why the management at financial institutions should read the book by all means.

I'm sure that the book gives a new perspective to the world of asset management.

11.Anonymous: financial media person 2

For the first time I encountered a book summarized so systematically and clearly.

Why do we need TSUMITATE INVESTMENT exactly now? — The question is squarely answered by the book of Mr. Yasuhira Hoshino.

In the global financial crisis in 2008, prices of all kinds of assets plunged, which made it hard to avoid asset erosion even in the case of diversified investments. How should investors prepare for such upheaval in financial markets? I think that one of the answers is TSUMITATE INVESTMENT, the subject of the book. With TSUMITATE INVESTMENT, positive returns can be achieved, even when the asset price falls by half. This part, which can be said as the most important point in the book, will give moral support to individual investors who are faced with the economic crisis once in one hundred years.

Insecurities, such as double-dip in the U.S. economy, European credit risk and monetary tightening in emerging economies, like China, the situation surrounding the global economy is increasingly becoming uncertain. However, readers of the book will understand that in this kind of environment right now, TSUMITATE INVESTMENT plays an effective role, which can increase assets without worrying about investment timings.

The contents of the book are based on the extensive research results of the author who did a lot of simulation. This is the first time for me to have encountered a book in which 'what TSUMITATE INVESTMENT is all about' is summarized so systematically and clearly. In this book, many new discoveries should be made by not only beginners but also people who have already some knowledge of TSUMITATE INVESTMENT. For example, the book points out, 'You don't have to be too careful about the timing to start TSUMITATE INVESTMENT, but watch out for the timing to end it'. This comment will be a very important piece of advice even for investors who have already started TSUMITATE INVESTMENT, especially investors in the US who are said to have a high level of financial literacy.

The past 10 years of the weak performance of the US stocks is called, 'lost decade'. In exactly such times, when stocks produce low returns, TSUMITATE INVESTMENT is important, the book teaches us.

Appendix B: Messages from Japanese Financial Planners and Bloggers

1. Choongdo Kang, SINYO FP Office

2. Kenichi Minase, A Random Walk Down Umeyashiki Street (Index Fund Investment Log)

3. Blogger "PET", Your Own Boss (Asset Management Blog)

4. mushitorikozou

5. Shunsuke Ito, Discussion on KYOUGOKU・DEMACHI Financial Planner

6. Tooru Ushiroda,"The Life Insurance Trap"

7. Blogger "Rakutenkagyou"

8. Blogger "TravelBookCafe"

9. Blogger "yako"

10. Blogger"I-no", An Ocean of Funds

11. Blogger "renny"

12. Blogger "Leverage", Leveraged Investment Diary

13. pockypocky

14. Blogger "m@"

15. Ryota Ito, Financial Planner

16. Blogger "taka"

17. Blogger "Jyuuichiya"

18. Blogger "makiko"

1. Choongdo Kang, SINYO FP Office

Whether or not you invest has nothing to do with your level of courage, it's merely about method.

Mr. Hoshino's "Tsumitate Investment" is an entirely new investment format that is the product of a Japan-style rearrangement of a Western concept.

In other words, you can steadily invest small amounts without making any huge, life-altering decisions and staying within the scope of your daily routine. Like the air you breathe, you invest just the right amount for you without over-exhaustion.

The appeal of tsumitate is the aspect of "automatic accumulation." A certain amount gets deducted from your bank account on a certain date every month to make purchases of mutual fund units.

Surprisingly, we don't have to pay anything for this system to work. Even if making 240 purchases over a 20-year time span, we pay no fees whatsoever. There is no easier way to invest than by automatic accumulation.

Such an easy-to-do, tailor-made investment method is bound to be widely accepted by investors around the world.

Choongdo Kang, President
SINYO FP Office: http://www.sinyo-fp.com/
Index fund investments that enrich your mind

2. Kenichi Minase, A Random Walk Down Umeyashiki Street (Index Fund Investment Log)

Lots happened over the years since I started tsumitate investing in an index fund.

—I started writing a blog about index fund tsumitate investing
—I became friends with other investors through my blog
—I participated in investment events organized by my investor friends
—I was interviewed by Money Magazine and various newspapers
—I was asked by asset management companies and securities exchanges to give my opinion
—Many people told me I should write a book and I did

What is obvious in Western countries, tsumitate investment in index funds, was merely reiterated in my blog and this is the result I got from the public. That's is how rare it was in Japan.

Compared to Western countries, Japan is still backwards in the area of financial products and tax systems for securities.

However, strong desires on the part of many investors have moved the investment climate gradually towards improvement. (Ex.) An increase in no-load funds, tsumitate investment services where a mutual fund investment plan can be started for as little as 1000 yen, among others.

I will stubbornly continue my own tsumitate investments in index funds while diffusing information to investors, securities firms and asset management companies.

Kenichi Minase, Index Fund Investment Blogger
http://randomwalker.blog19.fc2.com/

3. Blogger "PET", Your Own Boss (Asset Management Blog)

By investing a fixed amount every month without worry, tsumitate investing lets you use your time for yourself without wasting any by watching the markets fluctuate.

For a person like me suspicious of any type of investment scheme, tsumitate enables cool, stress-free asset formation in a way that matches my circumstances to a tee.

Although it's only been a few years since I started tsumitate investing, I want to continue long term over a period of several decades.

I would like to see this concept spread well beyond Japan's shores.

PET
http://amayaho.blog66.fc2.com/

4.mushitorikozou

In my interpretation, even small amounts of financial assets solely in the form of cash deposits is almost the same as a focused investment with its own inherent risks. This is why I have "tsumitate investments" consisting of international stocks and bonds that let me both maintain buying power and form assets.

Although it is impossible to perfectly predict the movements of the world's economies or monetary values, we can keep a good balance with respect to various aspects of the market by investing steadily in multiple types of assets. Theoretically, this would complement your main source of income.

I have too much to do and can't allocate time for investing. I have no spare time for watching the market. Tsumitate investing is neither advantageous nor disadvantageous. Rather, it is just beneficial enough without having to use any time or mental energy among all those investors around the world bent on getting rich at the expense of others. Long Live Tsumitate!

mushitorikozou
http://twilog.org/mushitori

5. Shunsuke Ito, Discussion on KYOUGOKU DEMACHI Financial Planner

It's not to make lots of money, it's so that I don't lose any. Because it's for assets in 10 or more years from now, I build them slowly and determinedly.

Even the longest journey begins with a single step.
Try tsumitate, you won't regret it. YATTEMINAHARE! (It's Japanese in the Osaka dialect meaning "Let's try!".)

Shunsuke Ito, Discussion on KYOUGOKU DEMATI Financial Planner
Get a second opinion for money matters too!
http://kyogokudemachifp.blog14.fc2.com/

6. Tooru Ushiroda, "The Life Insurance Trap"

I run an insurance agency and know that there's no insurance plan that beats having your own capital.

And tsumitate is a powerful tool at your disposal for fostering that capital.

From my perspective, it's disappointing that after recommending tsumitate investing to my customers I end up not making any money from it.

Tooru Ushiroda
http://www.seihosoudan.com/

7. Blogger "Rakutenkagyou"

From the viewpoint of a trader, tsumitate ＝ average down. However, the amount of the assets invested, the span and the method all differ in meaning.

Average down is a means to avoid losses.
It involves the short-term investment of a large amount in a single asset where the unit value is evenly decreased in an effort to recover any latent loss while bearing an excessive amount of risk.

However, tsumitate's main focus is the long-term contribution of a fixed amount paid monthly, dispersed into assets around the world and managed.

Because a drop in price is a chance to increase the purchase of units thus controlling latent losses, your stress is alleviated, tsumitate boasts psychological benefits providing a positive image to your investment activities.

However, from the perspective of investment profitability, notice that markets providing a return reversal effect are most likely to result in effective investments.

Therefore, considering time efficiency, such an investment method would be easy to accept by, for example, the office worker who is stably tsumitate investing under an asset allocation structure and receiving a stable income.

Rakutenkagyou, Individual investor
http://fpdiary.blog23.fc2.com/blog-entry-135.html

8. Blogger "TravelBookCafe"

"Tsumitate" is a word that symbolizes one of the characteristics of Japanese culture.

As witnessed in the aftermath of the recent Great Tohoku Pacific Coast Earthquake, the Japanese, all the while facing tremendous odds, will calmly and methodically act with discipline. The Japanese have overcome countless historical hardships through steady and continuous effort.

You'll never see a sumo wrestler grin happily and make high-fives when winning a match. Not displaying one's feelings even when happy is a trait handed down from the samurai.
It is a Japanese virtue to "live dispassionately, undeterred and sober."

The spirit of tsumitate was built upon this tradition.

Whether in bull or bear markets or during periods of high or low volatility, you continuously invest a fixed amount in a set frequency and approach your goal with a long-term view.

The concept behind tsumitate is none other than the spirit of Japan itself.

TravelBookCafe
http://d.hatena.ne.jp/travelbookcafe/

9. Blogger "yako"

Actually, the invention of tsumitate is a very recent thing.
I started my tsumitate investment some three years ago.

Before then, I always thought tsumitate was some kind of insurance policy because of the monthly "premiums".
*I remember when I was little, the insurance lady would come by the house every month to collect premiums in cash.

Now I have a tsumitate investment that combines Japanese stocks and bonds as well as foreign stocks (both from advanced and emerging countries) all in one fund.

There are three reasons:

-Japan was a "developing" country with regard to mutual funds, but finally we now able to diversify my investments using index funds for which we don't have to choose assets.

-We are now able to invest in global productivity little by little with small amounts.

-Because domestic bonds are not affected by exchange rates, I can have peace of mind by owning stable Japanese assets

It's important to focus on your own money for the future even if your income is different from others around you because of investing.

It's a lot of fun to manage your money in a way that let's you say to your money "get back here!" when you're old and gray...or "I missed you!" when it finds its way home from emerging markets and advanced countries.

yako
Blog: http://indexinvest.blog32.fc2.com/

10. Blogger"I-no", An Ocean of Funds

If you believe that capitalism will continue to develop, then invest in the market all the way through and become a big winner. Don't you agree that continuously investing little by little is the No. 1 way for the average person to participate in the market?

An Ocean of Funds   I-no Junichi
http://www.fund-no-umi.com/

11.Blogger "renny"

"From Drops of Dew to the Mighty River"   —   I love this phrase.

I continue my blog (http://renny.jugem.jp/: sorry, only in Japanese), which introduces my own investment and Japanese mutual funds for more than 5 years.

The reason why I continue blogging is that I would like to feel that "From Drops of Dew to the Mighty River" has been gradually and steadily realized by Japanese individual investors' tsumitate investment.

From my experience, I do not believe that a lot of Japanese people recognize that long-term investment has essentially very great power to bring comfortable life, pleasant time and surprisingly innovative solution to our everyday.

In the meanwhile, I also do believe that tsumitate investment surely make significant contribution to prevailing such a great power.

With regard to execution of tsumitate investment, I guess there is an important issue to be solved, which is the fact that it would be difficult for some people to constantly continue tsumitate investment.

As one of solutions for this important issue I set up a casual party in Tokyo, called '#k2k2 night,' together with Ms. Chiho Shimada and Ms. Minako Takekawa, because to have some friends, to whom we could frankly talk about money and individual financial plan, seems to be of good help.

Now this #k2k2 night is held every month. Additionally, the events similar to #k2k2 night has been organized at Yokohama, Sapporo, Okinawa, Hiroshima, Saitama, Osaka, Nagoya, and so on.The event in June 2011 will be 1st anniversary from the launch of #k2k2 night.

 I plan to continue this event as long as I can in order to realize "From Drops of Dew to the Mighty River" and, of course, I hope this idea of "From Drops of Dew to the Mighty River" and tsumitate investment will prevail all over the world.

renny
http://renny.jugem.jp/

12. Blogger "Leverage", Leveraged Investment Diary

Nobody can accurately forecast the direction the global economy. And instability has risen somewhat since we entered the 21st Century.

In these circumstances, tsumitate is an exceptional investment method from the point of view of behavioral finance stripping you of overconfidence and enabling you to have the peace of mind of the average individual investor and a constant dialogue with your wallet free of mental anguish.

Leverage
  "Leveraged Investment Diary" blog administrator
http://happy2020.cocolog-nifty.com/blog/

13.pockypocky

Greetings to all you investors around the world!
I have a question for you: Have you ever heard the word "tsumitate" before?

Please imagine a tall structure. Maybe a pyramid...
And let's say you want to climb up to the top of it.

But you can only go to the top using stairs. You can't zoom up there, you have to gradually escalate one stair at a time.
So what do you do when you reach the top?
Haven't you ever been surprised by the change in scenery just by elevating yourself somewhere?

In my analogy, replace the word "stairs" with "money" and the word "top" with your target amount.
Tsumitate is the action by which you can accumulate money towards that target.

Let's tsumitate together!
I look forward to the day when I can join hands with all the other investors in the world!

pockypocky
http://twilog.org/pockypocky

14. Blogger "m@"

Although you have no money now, you accumulate money little by little with a firm eye on a future goal.
You won't get some extravagant results, but this kind of investment is just right for the average person leading an average life.
You can enjoy your daily life while steadily building your nest egg.
Tsumitate investing should be used to brighten the lives of people around the world.

m@
http://ch01173.kitaguni.tv/

15. Ryota Ito, Financial Planner

I also have tsumitate investments and think that this concept of contributing a fixed amount every month even from as little as 10,000 yen is an easy way to invest, and continuing such a scheme indefinitely is optimal for anyone.

You never have to worry and just buy more units when the price goes down.

I believe that now is the time for more people to partake in such a wonderful concept.

For details, please read Mr. Hoshino's book.

Nobody knows when would be the best time to invest in order to ensure optimal performance. I hope the time will come when investors who contribute to plans that let them purchase assets little by little will sweep across the world of tomorrow.

Ryota Ito, Financial Planner
http://www.ryota-ito.jp/

16. Blogger "taka"

I have an index fund tsumitate investment because it lets me focus on my own work without worry and provides average results even though I am not a professional investor. This really appeals to me.

Investing is the foundation of our capitalism and free-market economy.
Tsumitate allows anyone to invest their own money globally without gloabally and effortlessly contributing to growth and sharing in profits.
Tsumitate, I learned about economics and finance.

I sincerely want more and more people to find out about tsumitate.

taka
http://freelikewind.blog72.fc2.com/

17.Blogger "Jyuuichiya"

I "tsumitate" for my future self.
When I retire far into the future, I will use little by little the money I accumulate now through "tsumitate" with a strong feeling of appreciation.

"Tsumitate" now is an act that will be appreciated by my future self.

I "tsumitate" for my present self.
My present self uses up lots of time for work, hobbies, investment, friends and family.
For me, "tsumitate" is optimal for investing globally without taking any time.

By "tsumitate" investing automatically a fixed amount each month, I can use the rest of my money for me.
My future self's money, my present self's money... only "tsumitate" can let me easily take control of it.

Jyuuichiya
http://39saku39saku.blog129.fc2.com/

18.Blogger "makiko"

Congratulations to publishing such booklet.
I know the "tsumitate" investment method doesn't make me wealth.

But it's simple and easy to start for anyone, especially for those whofear the investment.

Hope the word "tsumitate" will become a normal English word.
I believe it will be soon!

makiko
http://ameblo.jp/macky0108/

Appendix C: Date Summary

Chapter	Case	Answer	Total rate of return (%)	Investment Value ($)	Profit or loss ($)	Amount
1	Case 1: Even at half price	3	16.0%	13,924	1,924	2,785
	Case 2: Even after dipping to 10¢	3	21.2%	14,541	2,541	12,117
2	Case 3: When is the recovery?	1	1.1%	7,887	87	1,793
3	Case 4: Return to original level	3	101.2%	24,147	12,147	2,415
	Case 5: When it doubles	2	39.0%	16,686	4,686	834
4	Case 6: Going up, then dipping a little	2	4.7%	12,565	565	838
	Case 7: Return to original price	2	−26.5%	8,817	−3,183	882

Chapter	Case	Answer	Total rate of return (%)	Investment Value ($)	Profit or loss ($)	Amount
5	Case 8: When should I start?	3	130.9%	27,709	15,709	1,108
		1	133.7%	28,048	16,048	1,068
		2	133.3%	27,991	15,991	1,018
		4	128.3%	27,401	15,401	953
		5	117.1%	26,053	14,053	868
		6	102.9%	24,343	12,343	779
		7	92.0%	23,042	11,042	709
		8	83.4%	22,012	10,012	652
		9	76.4%	21,172	9,172	605
	Case 9: When should I start? (2)	9	56.4%	18,766	6,766	1,251
		7	77.5%	21,305	9,305	1,217
		5	99.0%	23,874	11,874	1,194
		3	118.2%	26,183	14,183	1,164
		2	130.9%	27,709	15,709	1,108
		1	133.3%	27,991	15,991	1,018
		4	117.1%	26,053	14,053	868
		6	92.0%	23,042	11,042	709
		8	76.4%	21,172	9,172	605
6	Case 10: Knowing when to stop is important	A	119.1%	26,288	14,288	657
		B	11.8%	13,415	1,415	671
7	Case 11: Even if your goals are the same	A	45.2%	17,420	581	5,420
		B	97.9%	23,744	791	11,744
	Case 12: The process is important	A	−10.5%	10,737	−1,263	215
		B	376.3%	57,153	45,153	1,143

TSUMITATE INVESTMENT: Lucrative even at half price

Chapter	Case	Ans wer	Total rate of return (%)	Investment Value ($)	Profit or loss ($)	Amount
8	Case 13: If periods vary	A	159.6%	31,157	19,157	312
		B	157.7%	61,855	37,855	619
		C	157.1%	92,555	56,555	926
9	Case 14: Slow increases	A	50.7%	18,081	6,081	181
		B	680.7%	93,681	81,681	937
	Case 15: What if it jumps 100 fold?	1	411.8%	61,421	49,421	61
10	Case 16: Vertically symmetric	A	4.7%	12,565	565	838
		B	16.0%	13,924	1,924	2,785
	Case 17: 8 zigzag funds	2	33.4%	16,006	4,006	800
		6	25.8%	15,095	3,095	839
		5	26.4%	15,169	3,169	892
		8	17.7%	14,124	2,124	942
		7	23.4%	14,803	2,803	987
		3	32.2%	15,867	3,867	1,058
		4	31.5%	15,785	3,785	1,127
		1	40.4%	16,843	4,843	1,203
	Case 18: Another 8 zigzag funds	1	22.8%	13,262	2,462	742
		3	17.4%	12,685	1,885	775
		4	17.4%	12,681	1,881	825
		8	11.3%	12,020	1,220	866
		7	12.8%	12,180	1,380	910
		5	16.9%	12,629	1,829	979
		6	14.9%	12,413	1,613	1,043
		2	18.0%	12,740	1,940	1,117

Appendix D: Translator Profile

John L. Clark

This booklet was translated from its original Japanese by Mr. John Clark, a Canadian business consultant with over ten years experience as a financial and legal translator in Tokyo. He was recruited for a teaching position in Niigata at age 21 back in 1994 and quickly decided to become a translator. After devising a unique method to study Japanese characters using newspaper articles and undergoing a two-year apprenticeship, he began his career translating instruction manuals for electronic devices and tourist booklets and over the years gradually moved up to legal contracts, prospectuses, depositions and securities reports. Mr. Clark is also a certified investment advisor and strongly believes in tsumitate investing as an effective asset formation method for the average consumer. He hopes his two beautiful children, Eri and Koki ("johnjohn") will grow up to become successful tsumitate investors!

http://www.standardconsulting.hk/